The Dynamics of Christian Unity

The Dynamics
of Christian Unity

A Symposium on the Ecumenical Movement
Compiled and Edited by

W. STANLEY MOONEYHAM
Editor, *United Evangelical Action*

ZONDERVAN PUBLISHING HOUSE
GRAND RAPIDS   MICHIGAN

Library of Congress Catalog Card No. 63-19721

Printed in the United States of America

INTRODUCTION

On December 7, 1948, the late Walter A. Maier appeared with a panel on a memorable radio broadcast over "The Town Meeting of the Air." The subject under discussion was, "Is a United Protestant Church Possible Now?" Declared Dr. Maier:

"Give us a united Protestant church; I ask you to pray for it. But let it be fully and honestly united in its acceptance of the faith once given, rooted in the Bible, and climaxed in Christ, the Son of God, and the Saviour of the world."

The originator of "The Lutheran Hour" believed that reformation would have to precede reunion. He said that American Protestantism could go forward to greater unity "only if it is ready to go back all the way to the Bible, and rededicate itself wholly to the full, free and final Gospel of Jesus Christ." He contended that where doctrines were in dispute, only a Scriptural verdict would suffice.

Since Dr. Maier's address, no full-dress effort has been made by a symposium to deal definitively with the subject of unity from a clear-cut evangelical point of view. Therefore it is a signal honor to be permitted to introduce this collection of studies to the reading public. The overwhelming desire of the contributors to seek unity and harmony in the Christian cause is evident from the opening page, and is the dominant and characteristic note of the entire volume.

Because I know these men, I know what they mean by unity in Christ. It is the most wonderful thing in the believer's life — a heartbond that is indefinable and yet tremendously evident. It transcends ecclesiastical barriers as easily as a bird soars over a church roof.

49733

I call the attention of these addresses particularly to my friends in the ecumenical movement. They deserve careful study, not because they are a final formulation of the evangelical position; for in fact they are only introductory studies. They deserve scrutiny because the issues that are raised here are issues that pierce to the very bone and marrow of contemporary discussions around the world. They cannot be dodged, and they will not lie down.

The authors have not attempted to point to any solutions other than the cross of Jesus Christ. They have not sought to bring all Christians under a single dogmatic umbrella. Sometimes they have made statements as individuals with which other evangelicals would disagree. I do not subscribe to every viewpoint represented in the work. Yet there is an unmistakable unity in the diversity here represented, and there is a love that passes understanding.

Hundreds of volumes have been written in our century on the subject of Christian unity. Here is a contribution that represents a very important area of the church—an area that is today setting the pace in evangelism, in missions, in parish outreach. It is primarily a message of love. May it travel far!

"Behold, how good and how pleasant it is for brethren to dwell together in unity! It is like ... the dew that descended upon the mountains of Zion: for there the Lord commanded the blessing, even life for evermore" (Psalm 133:1,3).

Sherwood E. Wirt, Editor
Decision Magazine
Minneapolis, Minn.

CONTRIBUTORS

DR. VERNON GROUNDS is the president of Conservative Baptist Theological Seminary, Denver, Colorado. His educational background includes the B.A. degree from Rutgers University, the B.D. degree from Faith Theological Seminary, and the Ph.D. from Drew University. He has been honored by membership in Phi Beta Kappa and by the Doctor of Divinity degree from Wheaton College.

DR. ARNOLD OLSON is the president of the Evangelical Free Church of America, Minneapolis, Minnesota. In this position he directs the overall efforts of the denomination in 35 states, five Canadian provinces and 13 district organizations. He is the author of two books and is an alumnus of Trinity College and Trinity Theological Seminary.

DR. EARLE E. CAIRNS is professor of history and chairman of the department of history at Wheaton College, Wheaton, Illinois. He is an ordained minister of the United Presbyterian Church, U.S.A., and holds his Bachelor of Theology from Presbyterian Theological Seminary. He was awarded his Master of Arts and his Doctor of Philosophy degrees at the University of Nebraska. He is the author of *Christianity Through the Centuries* and *Saints in Society*.

DR. CLYDE W. TAYLOR is director of public affairs of the National Association of Evangelicals and executive secretary of the Evangelical Foreign Missions Association, Washington, D.C. He has served in the nation's capital nearly twenty years after three terms as a missionary in South America. Frequent travels to all parts of the world make him a well-informed observer of missionary work abroad.

DR. GEORGE L. FORD is general director of the National Association of Evangelicals, Wheaton, Illinois. He was named to this position in 1963 after serving seven years as executive director and two years as associate executive director. He is an ordained minister of the Free Methodist Church, holds the A.B. degree from Los Angeles Pacific College and was awarded an honorary Doctor of Divinity degree by Greenville College. He is the author of *The Miracle of America.*

REV. W. STANLEY MOONEYHAM is director of information of the National Association of Evangelicals and editor of the official magazine, *United Evangelical Action.* He is a graduate of Oklahoma Baptist University and a former newspaperman. He later entered the ministry, served pastorates in Oklahoma and then was named executive secretary of the National Association of Free Will Baptists. He has been with the NAE since 1959.

TABLE OF CONTENTS

The Dynamics of Christian Unity

Chapter One

THE BIBLICAL BASIS OF CHRISTIAN UNITY

Vernon C. Grounds

As American evangelicals we are bearing witness to our faith in a time of unprecedented tension and crisis, an age of tantalizing potential as well as sinister threat. Within the orbit of Christendom, for example, surprising developments are taking place. None is more significant, however, than the ecumenical movement which the Episcopal Bishops in their September 1960 Pastoral Letter defined very succinctly:

> In simplest and broadest terms this is the movement at work among nearly all the separated companies of Christ's people throughout the world as they seek to overcome their separation one from another. Wherever it is found we see churches and bodies of Christians moving out of isolation into communication, out of competition into cooperation, out of estrangement into good will and understanding.[1]

Now ecumenism is founded on a single premise which the advocates of a unified church regard as self-evident and all-sufficient. According to the New Testament, they argue, Christians are one in essential faith; therefore Christians must strive to become one in structured fellowship. Spiritual oneness, in other words, must be embodied in some palpable reality, some organization which the non-Christian world can perceive and understand. Thus as Pope John XXIII said in his audience with the non-Catholic delegate-observers at the Second Vatican Council: "There burns in my heart the intention of working and suffering to hasten the hour when for all men the prayer of Jesus at the Last Supper will have reached its fulfillment, 'That they may all be one!' "[2]

That, then, is the purpose no less than the premise of the ecumenical movement: Christians who are one in faith must become one

---

[1] References are to be found at the end of the volume.

13

in fact, one in fellowship, one in visible organization. Failing that, the will of our Lord Jesus Christ will continue to be sinfully frustrated.

In ascertaining what the New Testament teaches with respect to the unity of the church, I want to answer a basic question: Does the unity of the church as taught in the New Testament justify the thrust of the ecumenical movement toward the eventual reunion of all churches within the orbit of Christendom? In answering this question we shall consider chiefly the *essential* unity of the church, with only a fleeting glance at its *empirical* unity and a still more fleeting glance in the direction of its *eschatalogical unity.* And since "dialogue" is the shibboleth of our day, I shall try to involve as many theologians as space permits.

But before we can focus on the matter of the church's essential unity, it is necessary that we have in mind at least a provisional concept of the church. What is this "x" quantity, this as yet unspecified something, which we are talking about? What is the church?

Unabashedly revealing my own sectarian bias, I quote a striking statement by that famous Baptist, Charles Haddon Spurgeon:

> I am in the truest sense a very sound churchman. I am, indeed, a high churchman; a most determined stickler for the church. I do not believe in salvation outside the pale of the church. I believe that the salvation of God is confined to the church, and to the church alone. You say, "What church?" God forbid that I should mean either the Baptist, the Independent, the Episcopalian, the Presbyterian, or any other church; I mean the church of Christ, the company of God's chosen, the fellowship of the blood-bought, be they where they may, for them is provided the feast of fat things. There is but one church in heaven and earth, composed of those called by the Holy Ghost, and made anew by his quickening power.[3]

Accuse me of sectarianism if you like, but please admit that Spurgeon's concept of the church is by no means sectarian. Not in the least! On the contrary, it expresses the mainstream conviction of Protestantism. The church is simply the company of all God's chosen, His elect, the spiritual fellowship of blood-bought believers, that vast host of men and women of every age, country, and denomination who have been called into the fellowship of Jesus Christ by the Holy Ghost and who by the Holy Ghost have been supernaturally regenerated. Accepting Spurgeon's concept as our working hypothesis, what can we say regarding the unity of the church?

We can say, and we ought to say, that the unity of the church is of its very essence. With the utmost emphasis we must say that the unity of the church is not a wistful ideal, a future hope; no, its unity is an indisputable fact. Now, today, at this very hour, despite its factions and schisms, the church of Jesus Christ is already one. Deny this and Paul's exhortation in Ephesians 4:3 is pointless: "Endeavor to keep the unity of the Spirit in the bond of peace." But affirm the existing unity of the church and Paul's exhortation makes probingly good sense. Thus the unity of the church is the datum from which we start; it is the truth which controls our thinking in this area. I reaffirm, consequently, that in its very essence the church of Jesus Christ is one; and the nature of its oneness is well stated in a famous hymn:

> We are not divided,
> All one body we,
> One in hope and doctrine,
> One in charity.

The church's oneness is not merely in the oneness of hope and charity and doctrine, crucial as they are; it is the oneness which springs from the church's deepest essence as the body of Jesus Christ. The importance of this truth is so immense that I suggest we examine it with care and thoroughness.

John 17 contains the high-priestly intercession of the Saviour. Verse 11 of that chapter contains the Magna Charta of the ecumenical movement: "And now I am no more in the world, but these are in the world, and I come to thee. Holy Father, keep through thine own name those whom thou hast given me, that they may be one, as we are."

We should also note verses 21 through 23: "That they all may be one; as thou, Father, art in me, and I in thee, that they also may be one in us: that the world may believe that thou hast sent me. And the glory which thou gavest me I have given them; that they may be one, even as we are one; I in them, and thou in me, that they may be made perfect in one; and that the world may know that thou hast sent me, and hast loved them, as thou hast loved me."

Now in this petition our Lord is pleading for a unity which only His redemptive passion could effect, a oneness akin to the oneness

within the Godhead — a spiritual oneness, of course, an organic oneness, a vital oneness which goes an infinity beyond any mere oneness of will or purpose or love. It is a oneness which the philosopher
might choose to call ontological, a oneness which exists under all
deceptive appearances to the contrary, an inalienable oneness of life
and being.

And this, I repeat, is the oneness which Jesus Christ has effected
by His redemptive passion, securing by His cross and suffering and
death the fulfillment of His own petition. Hence as individual after
individual across the centuries is given by the Father to the Son
through the Spirit, each of these believers is united with Jesus Christ
and thus united with all other believers in an indissoluble oneness
of life and being — a new cell in the growing organism of the church.

So in his book, *The Realm of Redemption,* Dr. J. Robert Nelson,
a leader in the ecumenical movement, has a pertinent passage concerning our Lord's high-priestly prayer:

> The implication of this petition reaches farther than the expres-
> sion of the Lord's wish for the Church. It says a great deal in a few
> words about the nature of this unity and says it very plainly. In the
> paraphrase by Alfred Loisy: "Christian unity is not merely a unity of
> purpose and a unity of means employed to effect this purpose, it is,
> rather, a vital organic union, not only similar to, but veritably identical
> with, the union of the Father and the incarnate Son." From the
> standpoint of Christian faith, no higher concept of the bond of unity
> among members of the Church than this, that they should represent
> on earth the unity existing between the Son and the Father, is possible.
> This is the profound mystery of the oneness of the Church, as incon-
> ceivable in its fullness as the manner of unity of the Holy Trinity.
> It is because the unity has such a supersensible basis in the divine
> nature that we must speak of it as being "given" by God, rather than
> created by man, and as being "preserved" by the Holy Spirit. To
> cite the appropriate parable of L. S. Thornton: "The unity of the
> Body is a living unity created and sustained by the one Spirit. The
> drenched soil holds together, whereas if left dry it would crumble
> apart into dust." The sole unifying power, which issues in the experi-
> ence of *koinonia* and binds together those who are by faith united in
> Christ, is that same divine relationship of the Trinity.[4]

Because the redemptive passion of Jesus Christ has secured and
is daily securing the fulfillment of His own petition, all believers are
already one: they are one in the sole way that our Saviour asked for
their unity. They may not be one organizationally, but they are one
organically. They may not be one structurally, but they are one

spiritually. They may not be one visibly, but they are one vitally. And that — and that alone, I venture to assert — is the burden of our great High Priest's intercession.

Yes, because of our Saviour's redemptive passion, His own petition is now finding daily fulfillment. Indeed, because of His passion, the children of God, scattered abroad are being gathered together in one, as Caiaphas unwittingly prophesied in John 11:52. Because of His passion, there is now one fold and one shepherd, as in John 10:16 our Shepherd Himself declared. There is now one vine into which all believers are branches, as we are told in John 15. There is now one household, one family, one brotherhood, as we read in Ephesians 2:19. There is now one temple, as Ephesians 2:21 discloses. There is now one bride, as Paul asserts in Ephesians 5. Because of our Saviour's passion, this unity now exists in answer to His own prayer. It does not lie in the future as expectation and promise; it does not lie in the realm of what is going to be; it lies in the here and now, the sphere of the present; it is a glorious reality, a reality which day by day is growing more and more glorious.

All of this comes to a focus in that remarkable metaphor, "the body of Christ," which Paul frequently uses. Notice I Corinthians 10:16-17: "The cup of blessing which we bless, is it not the communion of the body of Christ? For we being many are one bread, and one body: for we are all partakers of that one bread." Notice also I Corinthians 12:13: "For by one Spirit are we all baptized into one body, whether we be Jews or Gentiles, whether we be bond or free: and have been all made to drink into one Spirit." And notice likewise verse 27 of this chapter: "Now ye are the body of Christ, and members in particular."

Additional references, I take it, are superfluous. For Paul the church is the body of Jesus Christ. And it is the truth underlying this metaphor which enables the apostle to use another astonishing phrase — "in Christ." Very often that phrase appears in his writings — 164 times according to Adolph Deissman's tabulation. The phrase, "in Christ," Deissman states, is "the peculiarly Pauline expression of the most intimate possible fellowship of the Christian with the living spiritual Christ."[5]

But, on the other hand, Paul can simultaneously affirm, as in Galatians 2:20, that Christ is in every believer just as every believer is in Christ: "I am crucified with Christ: nevertheless I live; yet not I, but Christ liveth in me: and the life I now live in the flesh I live by the faith of the Son of God who loved me, and gave himself for me."

Now what bearing does all this have on the unity of the church? It impinges on that matter with overwhelming force. It means, very sharply put, that believers, since they are united organically to Jesus Christ, are united organically to one another. As members of the same Body, believers are indissolubly joined together in life and being. They compose, to quote Ernest Best, a corporate personality. And, to follow Dr. Best's exposition, the person who belongs to our Lord's body belongs primarily

> to a world-wide community, and only secondarily to a local mani-
> festation of it as a congregation in a particular place. When he travels
> he is always to be received in the local congregation as a brother in
> Christ. The individual congregation and denomination is therefore
> related to Christ, not directly, but because its members are members
> of the world-wide community which is in Christ and is his Body. The
> Church is not, consequently, to be described in terms of congrega-
> tions, but in terms of individual and interrelated Christians.[6]

"How then," Dr. Best asks, "shall we regard the Church?" And he answers:

> We have seen that it consists of a mass of interrelationships be-
> tween Christ and Christians, and between one Christian and another.
> This suggests that we should start by picturing it as a fellowship —
> a fellowship of Christians among themselves and with their Lord and
> Saviour who is the chief member of the fellowship.
> The note of fellowship — though a more closely knit, and more
> deeply experienced, fellowship than any earthly fellowship — is, conse-
> quently, the note of the Church. This fellowship must be distinguished
> from the mere gregariousness of a crowd; there, individuals lose their
> separate personalities in the whole; this is not so in the Church. It must
> also be distinguished from the mere possession of a common culture
> and a common set of purposes; it is, rather, a participation in the
> experiences of Christ and of other Christians. Christians died with
> Christ on the cross and they share in the new life of his resurrection.
> They are in him and so experience the redemption that God has
> wrought in him. As they have partaken of sin and death through
> Adam, so now they partake of life and righteousness through Christ.
> As Head of the Body, he supplies them with nourishment and energy.
> As members of his Body their movements are unified and they are
> built up in his love. In baptism they are made members of the fellow-
> ship. In the Eucharist they participate in him, and in one another.

They share sorrow and joy together. One suffers that another may be comforted. By what each endures the whole Church is built up. If one fails to grow, the growth of the whole is hindered. That is the uniform evidence of the New Testament; even as soon as the company of believers is first mentioned, "fellowship" is picked out as its distinctive feature (Acts 2:42-47; 4:32-37).[7]

Now three far-reaching corollaries follow from Paul's teaching that every believer as a member of Christ's Body sustains a direct relationship to his Saviour and is accordingly united indissolubly to every other believer. For one thing, the Pauline doctrine of the church refutes the common ecumenical argument that somehow separated denominations lacerate our Lord's body. J. Marcellus Kik deals effectively with this contention:

> The body exists as an organic whole — *we, being many, are one body; there is one body; as the body is one; by one Spirit are we all baptized into one body; now ye are the body of Christ.* Most scholars agree that an overall organization did not exist in the first century church; yet the apostle teaches clearly that one body did exist. Because individual or groups of churches have separate organizations does not imply a fragmentation of the body of Christ. Paul also uses the figure of the temple to indicate the organic oneness of the Church, "In whom all the building fitly framed together groweth unto an holy temple in the Lord: in whom ye also are building together for an habitation of God through the Spirit" (Eph.2:21, 22). The fundamental idea of this text is that the Church constitutes an organic totality. The possibility of a fragmented body because of separate organizations is an absurd idea as one grasps the fundamental significance of the figure used by Paul.[8]

For a second thing, the Pauline doctrine of the church, refutes the common ecumenical argument that unity must eventually be organizational. Again I turn to Dr. Kik for rebuttal of this unfounded assumption:

> The body achieves unity through union with Christ. Because the Church is one body in Christ, believers become members one of another. "We, being many, are one body in Christ, and every one members one of another." The body is knit together by the Head. From Christ the whole body is fitly joined together. Paul's conception of unity is not related to polity but is ontologically motivated — unity belongs to the very essence of the Church. The Church is conceived as a collective personality. Unity exists — otherwise the body does not exist. Unity is not contingent on organization but on union with Christ.[9]

For a third thing, the Pauline doctrine of the church refutes the common ecumenical argument that participation in the visible church and its sacraments apparently suffices to guarantee redemption. Let me appeal to Dr. Kik one more time:

> Bishop Newbigin . . . tries to establish the paradox of sin and holiness in the believer to be the paradox of the visible church. "That paradox, familiar to every Christian, is perhaps the simplest way of expressing the paradox of the Church's being" (*The House-hold of God,* p. 143). He maintains that Luther's doctrine of justification by faith for the individual should be applied to the corporate, visible church. He writes, "But if this is true, then Luther abandoned his deepest insight when he substituted for the true, biblical picture of a Church both holy and sinful, a false and unbiblical distinction between the spiritual church and the material Church or between the invisible Church and the visible Church. Both of these related pairs of terms have the effect of relaxing the true eschatological tension which is involved in recognizing that in Christ we, along with all our brethren, are accepted as His while we are yet sinners, and of substituting an essentially legalistic and pharisaic conception that some are — so to say — in the Church by right and others only by grace" (ibid., p. 143).

> What Bishop Newbigin implies is that the visible church is saved in its entirety. Those who receive the external rites of the church are *ipso facto* members of the body of Christ. It is a known fact that within the visible church there are those who deny the fundamental doctrines of the Christian faith and those who live immoral lives. Paul speaks pointedly to the Corinthian church, "Know ye not that the unrighteous shall not inherit the kingdom of God" (I Cor. 6:9). Jesus in the Sermon on the Mount denies entrance to the Kingdom to those who had not lived according to the will of God though they had made profession of faith. As Paul states in the eighth chapter of Romans, "Now if any man have not the Spirit of Christ, he is none of his." Neither Christ nor the apostles equate the visible church with the body of Christ.[10]

In short, salvation is not guaranteed to members of any visible church merely on the ground of that membership. Even if ultimately the ecumenical dream comes true and there is just one Christian church in the entire world, membership in that church will be no guarantee of salvation any more than membership in our churches today. Salvation is guaranteed only to members of the church which can never be fragmentized — and that is our Saviour's body.

With the Pauline concept of the church in mind, we return to his definitive statement of essential unity at the beginning of Ephesians 4. And what is the gist of the apostolic statement? Unity already exists as the work of the Triune God, each member of whom is succinctly mentioned. Verse four teaches that by the ministry of the

Holy Spirit every believer now belongs to the same Body and possesses the same hope of future beatitude. Verse five teaches that every member of Christ's Body has trustingly accepted the same Saviour and expressed his trust by the same ordinance. Verse six teaches that every member of that one Body has been chosen by the same God who omnipotently guides and blesses. Hence every believer is admonished to preserve this unity created by Father, Son, and Holy Spirit, a unity independent of any visible or human organization.

May I add a parenthesis here? In this Ephesian statement on unity Paul stresses a common faith — the apostolic deposit of doctrine, as I interpret it — and he totally ignores organizational oneness. How ironic it is, then, that the ecumenists as a rule turn Paul upside down! They ignore doctrine, they minimize the apostolic deposit of faith, and emphasize a structural oneness about which Paul says nothing. Am I exaggerating? Listen to Leslie Newbigin:

> The true character of this union of believers with one another in Christ is disastrously distorted when it is conceived of essentially in terms of doctrinal agreement. The effect of such distortion is to break the Christian fellowship up into rival parties, each based upon some one-sided doctrinal formulation, and eventually into completely separated bodies.[11]

And Charles Clayton Morrison predicts that in the united church of the future there will be doctrinal diversity instead of soul-shackling uniformity!

> Our present thesis is that the inmost structure of the united church can have no formal standards of loyalty save the authority inherent in the Lordship of Christ, and that the entire subject matter of the sectarian standards must be given its place in the freedom of its fellowship.[12]

What a travesty of the New Testament! Organizational unity which Paul ignores purchased at the price of doctrinal unity which he stresses! As I read the New Testament, however — to sum up this aspect of our study — the unity of the church has nothing to do with that centralized, monolithic, visible, global organization which the great majority of ecumenists hope to create. The unity of the church is a glorious reality which the Triune God has already created — a unity of persons created by divine purpose, passion and power.

Let us, therefore, take only a fleeting glance at a second aspect of our study, the church's *empirical* unity. Granted that the church is essentially one. Granted, in other words, that its unity in Jesus Christ is of the church's very essence. Have we no responsibility to strive for any visible manifestation of that oneness? Undoubtedly we have! Is it necessary for me to belabor something so obvious? The church is positionally holy in Jesus Christ, yet that fact does not release us from the obligation of trying to make our churches empirically holy. In precisely parallel fashion, though the church already is indissolubly one in Jesus Christ, it is our obligation to unify our churches empirically as much as lies within human ability. To churches corporately, as much as to believers personally, the New Testament imperative bindingly applies: Become what you are! As J. Robert Nelson admonishes us:

> The fact that the unity of the Church is "given" or created by God in the very constituting of the Body of Christ need not and should not deceive men into thinking that they have no responsibility for the Church's unity. On the contrary, the Christians' responsibility on behalf of unity is very great, for it is their task to *express* the unity, rather than to create or achieve it. This is why it is not accurate in the ecumenical movement to speak of "building the unity of the Church" or of "unifying the church," except in so far as order and organization are concerned. The proper word in this worldwide movement is "reunion" — the reassembling of the divided and scattered hosts of the People of God into the state of mutual recognition, common faith, *koinonia, and love.* These are the expressions of unity, not the tools and materials by which it is made. In the light of this existing, though repressed, unity of the Church, the keynote of divided Christians is the dictum: Become what you are, not what you hope to be. Unless there lies deeply embedded in the faith of Christians this conception of unity as a fundamental gift of God to be expressed and used, rather than as a goal to be attained, the prospects for a Church which maintains "the unity of the Spirit in the bond of peace" are most discouraging.[13]

Well and good! But how is the essential unity of the church to be expressed empirically? Does this require organizational oneness? Does it demand some sort of centralized government, a world-embracing structure, a monolithic super-church which includes all the churches now in existence? Is it only thus that unity can find adequate expression empirically? Absolutely not! As a matter of fact, loyalty to the New Testament may compel us to fight against organizational unity. For what does the New Testament teach? Does it teach that denominational plurality contradicts spiritual unity? Bishop Newbigin contends that it does. So he ringingly avers:

They do not grapple with the fact, which any serious reading of the New Testament must surely make inescapable, that to speak of a plurality of Churches is strictly absurd; that we can only do so insofar as we have ceased to understand by the word "Church" what the New Testament means by it; that our ecclesiologies are, in the Pauline sense, carnal.[14]

But is Newbigin right? Does the spiritual oneness of the church rule out organizational plurality? Is a diversity of denominations absurd and carnal? Over against the bishop's pronouncement let me put the verdict of Dr. R. W. Dale, that judicious Congregationalist whose reputation as a theologian is still deservedly very high:

There is nothing in the New Testament to suggest that the apostles intended that separate Christian assemblies should be drawn into a larger ecclesiastical organization under a central government. The church at Jerusalem had no control over the church at Antioch; nor were Jerusalem and Antioch under the government of any supreme ecclesiastical authority. The churches which Paul and Barnabas founded in Lycaonia, Pisidia, and Pamphilia on their first missionary journey were independent of the church at Antioch and each other. In every city there was a church, and in every church there were elders (Acts 14:21-23), but the narrative of Luke gives the impression that every church stood apart. No attempt was made to bring them into any ecclesiastical confederation or to place them under a common government. In the account of Paul's second visit to this part of Asia Minor we are told that the "churches" — not "the church" — "were strengthened in the faith and increased in numbers daily" (Acts 16:5). They were standing apart still, and Paul did nothing to draw them together.[15]

If Dale is right and Newbigin wrong — and I for one side with Dale — then loyalty to the New Testament does not necessitate organizational union. Quite the reverse! It warrants a continued plurality of churches.

Whenever ecumenists stridently denounce the incompatibility between spiritual oneness and organizational diversity, I think of what Charles Hodge has to say on this score — and surely he does not require an introduction to evangelicals.

As independent or separate organization is admitted to be consistent with true unity, by all but Romanists, it follows that any reason not destructive of the principle of unity, may be made the ground of such separate organization; not merely difference as to location, or diversity of language, but diversity of opinion. It is on all hands conceded that there may be difference of opinion, within certain limits, without violating unity of faith; and it is also admitted that there may be independent organization, for considerations of convenience, without violating the unity of communion. It therefore follows, that where such a diversity of opinion exists, as to render such separate organization convenient, the unity of the church is not violated by such separation. Diversity of opinion is indeed an evidence of imperfection, and therefore such separations are evil, so far as they are evidence of want of perfect union in faith. But they are a less evil than either hypocrisy or contention; and therefore, the diversity of sects, which exists in the Christian world, is to be regarded as incident to imperfect knowledge and imperfect sanctification. They are to be deplored, as every other evidence of such imperfection is to be regretted, yet the evil is not to be magnified above its just dimensions. So long as unity of faith, of love, and of obedience is preserved, the unity of the church is as to its essential principle safe.[16]

I heartily agree with Dr. Hodge — and in agreeing with a Presbyterian I am displaying a truly ecumenical attitude! We can manifest spiritual unity regardless of continued organizational diversity. We can manifest it by fellowship together, worship together, study together, prayer together, witness together, service together, and perhaps suffering together. We can manifest it by a voluntary cooperation which cuts across all denominational lines. And such voluntary cooperation is far more spiritual in every respect than a coerced and compromising union which violates conscience.

At the same time, however, let us remember that the manifestation of our spiritual unity is a God-imposed obligation. Let us remember the example of Paul who, as Oscar Cullman properly emphasizes, was ready

to make sacrifices for the sake of unity; sacrifices for those whom he designated as "weak in the Faith." To them he gave up his freedom in the question of the observance of the law. He did not wish that a brother who had not yet come very far, should take offence in the fact that he could be treated with contempt over certain ritual food regulations. We must read everything he writes concerning the strong and the weak in the First Epistle to the Corinthians and especially in Romans 14. "For the sake of food, do not destroy the work of God" (Rom. 14:20). A lasting unity is not possible in any community without effort and that is true of the Church also. Paul knew that. For this reason, he directly admonishes the strong to place love above their freedom in affairs of ritual. The unity of the Church is not possible without effort, effort for the brethren for whom Christ died, as Paul says in this connection (Rom. 14:15). He himself knew how to be a Greek for the Greeks and a Jew for the Jews. We learn from the Acts of the Apostles that during his last visit to Jerusalem, he even took a so-called

"Nazarite vow." Whenever we speak of the ecumenical problem, we should certainly take this aspect into consideration. For all speaking for the unity of the church and indeed our prayers can be in vain where there does not exist a readiness to make an effort in love for this unity.[17]

Let us remember Paul's example, and remembering it let us strenuously endeavor not alone to maintain our spiritual oneness but to manifest it empirically in every conceivable way.

Since we are engaged in dialogue, I conclude this phase of our discussion with a passage of penetrating discernment from the third volume of Emil Brunner's systematic theology, *The Christian Doctrine of the Church, Faith and Consummation*. The union of the Protestant Churches, he contends,

is impossible, because they embody irreconcilable, antithetical formative principles. It will never be possible to unite the Baptist or Congregationalist Churches with the Episcopalians, because in the one case and the other the formative principles and ideals, that of the autonomous congregation and of the Church under central leadership, stand in irreconcilable conflict with each other. This insuperable hindrance, both in the Confessional conflict (Catholic-Protestant) and in the denominational one (Baptists-Episcopalians), lies in the fact that in both cases the institution is identified with the Ekklesia. Such an identification is, however, neither necessary nor justified. The Protestant Churches all recognize the primitive form of the Ekklesia as the New Testament ideal, which is implied in the understanding of faith, that is, in Christology, and is normative for the Church.

But, as we have seen, the Ekklesia itself is certainly not a Church in the institutional sense, but a brotherhood resulting from faith in Christ. If this fact were acknowledged, at least by the Churches which sprang from the Reformation, the stumbling block caused by the multiplicity of Churches and the spiritual reasons for having one Church would disappear. Interest would turn away from the form of the Church and towards our common service. Each Church would see that its special form can very well be regarded as a special means for accomplishing our common service. Institutional organization would be regarded from the first as of merely relative importance. When every Church sees that it *is not* the Body of Christ, but only *serves* to build up that Body, the differences are made relative, and are freed from the pressure of the New Testament Ekklesia-norm. Each Church could then very well regard the others as so many instruments or vessels which serve the one purpose, the creation of true fellowship in Christ, of true Ekklesia.[18]

Reading Brunner's prescription for empirical unity among Christians, what can an evangelical do but endorse it with enthusiasm?

Finally, let us glance very fleetingly at the matter of the church's eschatological unity. For as Dr. Nelson admits and insists, complete oneness cannot be achieved in this world. No matter how successful the ecumenical movement may be, complete oneness can be achieved only in the world to come.

> Since this full unity has never been thoroughly realized, however, being from the time of the apostles a hoped-for expression of unity rather than a present possession, the question remains open, whether complete unity can be realized in history, or whether it belongs to the eschatological destiny of the Church. It is not sufficient to discuss the Church's unity without bearing in mind how relevant to it is the expectation of ultimate consummation in the Kingdom of God. "If the given unity of the Church is essentially eschatological," writes T. F. Torrance, "then the validity of all that she does is conditioned by the *Parousia* and cannot be made to repose upon any primitive structure of unity already complete in the natural parallel historical realm or upon any continuity in the fallen world out of which we are redeemed." However successful our efforts at outward reunion may be, however genuine the spiritual union of all Christians, however real the unity of the Church with Christ—these all have an ultimate point of reference which is transcendent and eschatological. It is eschatology which gives to the Church its form of unity, remarks G. Gloege, since unity is bound to the Christian hope for the fulfillment of God's rule. So we must seek the continuation of this discussion in the problem of the relation of the Church to the Kingdom of God.[19]

Need we deny this? By no means! We must affirm it vigorously because the New Testament does. Three facts will suffice to convince us, I am sure, that the unity of the church can be achieved in perfection only eschatologically. First, though the church is already one in Jesus Christ, the whole church has not yet been gathered unto Him in faith. Some of its members are still missing because as yet they do not believe or because as yet they have not been born. Second, you and I who belong to the Church Militant here on earth are exiled from the immediate presence of our Lord as well as cut off from personal fellowship with the Church Triumphant. Third, as members of the Church Militant we are not joined together in complete harmony of mind and heart and love and purpose; a few jarring discords mar the symphony of Christian communion. And when these discords have been resolved, new ones will develop. Rest assured of that.

But a day is coming when the Church will be perfectly one. A day is coming when all God's people will be united forever in face to face beatitude with their Lord and in harmonious fellowship with one another.

And in that day our Saviour's petition in John 17:24 will be fully granted, "Father, I will that they also, whom thou hast given me, be with me where I am; that they may behold my glory, which thou hast given me: for thou lovedst me before the foundation of the world."

Chapter Two

SCHISMATIC OR SEPARATIST?

Vernon C. Grounds

When any church tolerates either heresy or immorality of a flagrant character, what ought a Christian do? Suppose his prayer and protest have been unavailing? What is the course of action he ought to follow?

The New Testament gives him an unambiguous mandate, a mandate which has been obeyed by the greatest theologians in Protestantism when they faced such situations. The conscientious Christian in obedience to the Word of God ought to leave the disobedient church to which he belongs and seek a new fellowship which is obedient to divine truth.

But many Christians, even though they aspire to obey their God, hesitate to take so drastic a step. They are extremely reluctant to become separatists. Why? To become a separatist, it seems, is to become a schismatic, and schism is a terrible sin.

So a conscientious Christian may find himself painfully impaled on the horns of dilemma. To remain in his disobedient church is evil — unquestionably so. To be guilty of schism, however, is also an evil, and probably a worse evil than to remain in his disobedient church. Hence he chooses what impresses him as the lesser of the evils. Far better to tolerate the heresy and immorality in his church than to commit the sin of schism.

In electing this horn of his dilemma a conscientious Christian discovers that he is in excellent company indeed. He joins Chrysostom, the Greek theologian of the fifth century, who declared, "To make a schism in the Church is no less evil than to fall into heresy,"[1] and who also asserted, "Nothing angers God so much as the division of the Church. Even if we have done ten thousand good deeds, those of us who cut up the fulness of the Church will be punished no less than those who cut his body"[2] — a reference to the literal laceration of our Lord's flesh on Calvary.

The Christian who elects to tolerate some evil in his church, even flagrant evil, rather than to perpetrate the evil of schism is adopting in his day the position taken by Augustine, the famous fifth century bishop of Hippo, who borrowed many of his arguments from Cyprian, the third century bishop of Carthage. Pleading on behalf of Mother Church, Augustine writes to the Donatists, a notorious sect of his time: "What have I, your mother, done to you? I expel the evil ones when I am able; those whom I cannot expel I am compelled to tolerate. I tolerate them either until they are healed, or until they are separated at the last."[3]

Toleration of evil within the church is necessary, Augustine argues, for, if a zealous believer attempts to separate the wheat from the chaff, he unlovingly breaks the unity of God's family and arrogantly usurps the prerogative of Jesus Christ to whom alone the right of judgment belongs. The wheat and the tares must grow together until the Lord comes. Meantime the disciple's task is to keep himself pure, not to purify the church; no, the church throughout its history will remain a mixture of good and bad, hypocrisy and genuineness, exactly as the New Testament has foretold. Why, then, sacrifice unity and charity for an impossible purity?

Furthermore, in electing to tolerate unbelief or immorality rather than to risk schism, the conscientious Christian is at one with John Wesley. In a noted sermon, entitled "On Schism," the founder of Methodism states forthrightly that separation from "a body of living Christians, with whom we were before united," is "a grievous breach of the law of love."[4]

Though Wesley's societies grew restive within the framework of Anglicanism, he doggedly combated any move in the direction of separatism. In 1744 during a colloquium with some of his followers he was asked: "Do you not entail a schism in the Church? that is, Is it not probable that your hearers, after death, will be scattered into all sects and parties; or that they will form themselves into a distinct sect?" With typical thoroughness and candor Wesley replied:

(1) We are persuaded the body of our hearers will even after our death remain in the Church, unless they be thrust out.

(2) We believe notwithstanding, either that they will be thrust out; or that they will leaven the whole Church.

(3) We do, and will do, all we can to prevent those consequences which are supposed likely to happen after our death.

(4) But we cannot with a good conscience neglect the present opportunity of saving souls while we live, for fear of consequences which may possibly or probably happen after we are dead.[5]

Yet Wesley was acutely aware of the difficulties in his position. In 1788 he made this entry in his *Journal*:

> I fain would prevent the members here from leaving the church; but I cannot do it. As Mr. Gibson is not a pious man, but rather an enemy to piety, who frequently preaches against truth, and those that hold it and love it, I cannot with all my influence persuade them either to hear him, or to attend the sacrament administered by him.[6]

And one year later in his "Farther Thoughts on Separation from the Church," Wesley affirmed flatly concerning ministers who were not preaching the gospel: "I believe, to separate thus far from these miserable wretches, who are the scandal of our Church and nation, would be for the honour of our Church, as well as to the glory of God."[7]

In our own day, therefore, many conscientious believers hesitate to obey the New Testament directive regarding separatism for the same reasons which caused Chrysostom, Augustine, and Wesley to tolerate evil rather than commit the sin of schism — that "most horrible sacrilege" as Augustine branded it.[8]

The case against separatism, consequently, must be examined carefully, its full strength unflinchingly gauged. What specifically are the arguments which have been advanced by the protagonists of the anti-separatist position?

First, separatism is allegedly a wrong-headed, wrong-hearted sin against authority. This argument goes back to Tertullian, who in the second century helped to lay the foundations of Roman Catholic ecclesiology. To quote S. L. Greenslade, Tertullian advocated an hierarchical Christianity which fused inseparably authoritarianism and institutionalism:

> That doctrine is binding and catholic which is apostolic; it is found in apostolic writings and in the apostolic tradition of those Churches which have a continuous historical identity from apostolic times. The succession of bishops in such a see is the outward proof of its continuity; the bishops themselves are the appointed guard-

ians of apostolic truth. There is a fixed *regula fidei*, and Tertullian discusses with anxious care such phrases as "Search the Scriptures" and "Seek and ye shall find," which speculative heretics pleaded in self-defence . . . Order and authority are to him necessary conditions of *pax*, unity.[9]

In short, a separatist who pits his own Spirit-guided interpretation of Scripture against the teaching of the church is disobeying the authority which has been divinely established.

While he totally repudiates the Roman Catholic concept of the church, Edward John Carnell maintains that it was the sin of disobeying authority which turned J. Gresham Machen into a schismatic when the latter set up "The Independent Board for Presbyterian Foreign Missions" rather than support the official missionary agency which he charged had modernists in it. When the General Assembly ordered the board dissolved, Machen disobeyed the order.

Carnell holds that quite invariably separatism degenerates into schism because the proper authority of the church is flouted by the separatist.

Perhaps to this charge a Protestant can only answer with Martin Luther that ultimately he acknowledges no authority other than the authority of Scripture. There is a pseudo-authority which a Christian must disobey in order to obey God as He commands through His Word. That learned seventeenth century Congregationalist, John Owen, explained why it was not sinful to leave the Anglican fellowship:

> The Church of England as it is called separated herself from the Church of Rome . . . In her designe to reduce Religion to its primitive purity, shee always professed, that shee did not take direction from the Scripture only, but also from the Councells and examples of the four or five first Centuries . . . What I beseech you shall bind my Conscience to acquiesce in what is pleased from the 4 or 5 first Centuries consisting of men, that could, and did erre; more than did hers, what was pleaded from the 9 or 10 Centuries. Have I not liberty to call for Reformation according to the Scriptures only.[10]

Second, separatism is allegely a wrong-headed, wrong-hearted sin against humility. This obviously is a corollary of the sin against authority. For it is only inflated presumption which will motivate an individual to defy the authority of his church. All too often, then, what lies at the bottom of separatism? Pride!

Chrysostom, then, was not overly harsh when he said, "Nothing will so avail to divide the church as love of power."[11] Refusing to submit himself to God's surrogates, a separatist highmindedly strives to be a law unto himself. He even usurps the place and function of Jesus Christ as Judge! So Cyprian, in a passage cited by Dr. Carnell, rebukes this antithesis of humility:

> Although tares, or impure vessels, are found in the church, yet this is not a reason why we should withdraw from it. It only behooves us to labor that we may be the wheat, and to use our utmost endeavors and exertions, that we may be vessels of gold or of silver. But to break in pieces the vessels of earth belongs to the Lord alone, to whom a rod of iron is also given. Nor let any one arrogate to himself what is exclusively the province of the Son of God, by pretending to fan the floor, clear away the chaff, and separate all the tares by the judgment of man. This is proud obstinacy and sacrilegious presumption, originating in a corrupt frenzy.[12]

Third, separatism is allegedly a wrong-headed, wrong-hearted sin against unity. Rarely, if ever, has this argument been more powerfully presented than by Cyprian, who in work after work denounces the sacrilegious nature of schism. Here, conveniently, is a synopsis of his position made by G. G. Willis:

> The Nicene Creed professes the Christian belief in one holy catholic apostolic Church; and for Saint Cyprian this unity of the Body of Christ is clearly demonstrated to be the will of our Lord not only by the stress laid upon it in his great high-priestly intercession on the night of his Passion, but also by the fact that the divine promise of the indefectibility of the Church was first given to one man, Saint Peter, and then later to the other Apostles. Moreover, after the Resurrection, Saint Peter was himself charged to feed the flock of Christ. Since this unity is the will of God, nobody who is outside it can be considered sure of salvation; and so we have the clear principle which has for centuries been used as the succinct statement of his view, "extra ecclesiam nulla sallus." (Outside the church no salvation) . . . For the House of God is one, and outside it none can be safe. In the old law he who would not obey the priest was slain with the temporal sword: to be cast out of the Church now, for disobedience to the bishops, is to be slain with the spiritual sword . . . To separate oneself from the divinely ordained unity is to renounce Christ, to bear arms against his Church, to militate against the disposition of God. It is to do something at once illicit and destitute of all authority. It constitutes spiritual whoredom, which will separate a man from God and exclude him from eternal salvation. The man who initiates schism

rends the seamless robe of Christ. Schism does not indeed divide the Church, which is essentially indivisible, but it separates its authors from the Church, and puts them in the position of apostates. These are natural and inevitable judgments according to the rigid view of unity held by Saint Cyprian. For him schism is the mark of pride, selfishness and partisan feeling, just as unity is the outcome and manifestation of charity. . . . Saint Cyprian illustrates his view from Scripture by reference to the seamless robe of Christ of which mention has already been made, to the words of the Psalmist who describes God as "making men to dwell of one mind in an house," to the mission of the Holy Ghost in the form of a dove, the creature at peace, at Christ's baptism, and finally to the choice of bread and wine as outward signs of the blessed sacrament, signifying by the compacting of many grains of wheat into bread, and the compression of the juice of many grapes into wine, the unity of the Church of Christ.[13]

Even if one disagrees with Cyprian exegetically and theologically, he cannot disagree with him pragmatically. Once the disruptive process begins, it gains momentum irresistibly. Repudiate the church's authority, let every Christian be his own pope, and anarchy ensues. Hence Carnell is merely reporting what has happened and what is still happening: "an endless proliferation results."[14] Separatism leads to a mushrooming of minuscule, hairsplitting sects. This is confessedly a grievous weakness of Protestantism, yet it may be the inescapable concomitant of spiritual freedom and virility. It is a weakness which can be mitigated, however, by copying the spirit of those Congregationalists who withdrew from the Second Parish in Ipswich, Massachusetts, during the 1740's:

We can truly say, that we dislike Separations on trivial and flighty Reasons, as much as any Christians, and would with Humility caution against such, or of taking Example by us, to separate without weighty Reasons: But where Christians are treated by the Churches and Pastors, as we have been treated by ours, we have Freedom to say, that we have no great Concern about preserving the outward Peace of such Churches; and we think it highly offensive to God if they do not separate, since we can't see what Gospel End can be served, for Persons to be held down under spiritual Tyranny, in order to support and maintain such a Peace.[15]

Finally, separatism is allegedly a wrong-headed, wrong-hearted sin against charity. On this matter Augustine in his prolonged controversy with the Donatists said much which is of enduring value:

Essential grace is lacking . . . to all those outside the Church, and what is lacking is the crown of Christian virtues, without which all other virtues are as "sounding brass and a tinkling cymbal," the grace of charity, the first of the Spirit's fruits. Charity is the proper gift of Catholic unity and peace. The man who is destitute of it, and separates himself from the unity of the Church, is sunk in the darkness of schism by losing the light of charity. Until he repossesses charity, no other gift in baptism or in any other sacrament or means of grace is of any use, though they may be held in suspense, as it were, until, by virtue of his unity with the Body of Christ, they revive and become for the first time profitable to salvation. That is the appeal which Augustine makes to the separated Africans, and in all this wearisome controversy he longs continually for the peace of the City of God, reunited in the bond of charity.

> We shall be, as it were, in a city—brethren, when I speak of it, I would fain speak on for ever, especially when offences multiply. Who would not long for that city whence no friend goes out, where no enemy enters, where there is no tempter, no stirrer of faction, no divider of the people of God, no harasser of the Church in the Devil's service?

For the root and persistence of schism is nothing else than hatred of the brethren.[16]

Who will presume to challenge the great bishop's contention? Schism is usually harsh, intolerant, denunciatory, judgmental, and vindictive. Born of pride, it is the enemy of love, filling the churches with hate. Why not frankly recognize this peril and constantly keep in mind that, if separatism degenerates into a love-negating schism, it is indefensibly sinful?

Certainly schism is an evil, a pestilential evil. Certainly, also, separatism has sometimes degenerated into schism and can still so degenerate. But need schism and separatism be equated or is there a legitimate separatism which is not schismatic?

Let us resort once again to John Owen, that Puritan giant whose theological insight renders his judgment timelessly pertinent.

> I am most certain that a Separation from some Churches true or pretended so to be is commanded in the Scripture; so that the withdrawing from, or relinquishment of any Church or society whatever, upon the plea of its corruption, be it true or false, with a mind and resolution to serve God in the due observation of Church institutions, according to that light which men have received, is no where called Schisme, nor condemned as a thing of that nature. ...[17]

And to quote William Chillingworth, another giant of that same remarkable age when Puritanism and Congregationalism were impugning an Anglicanism not thoroughly reformed:

Neither is it always necessity schismaticall to separate from the externall Communion of a Church, though wanting nothing necessary. For if this Church . . . require me to professe against my conscience, that I beleeve some error, though ever so small and innocent which I doe not beleeve, and will not allow me her Communion but upon this condition; In this case the Church for requiring this Condition is Schismaticall, and not I for separating from the Church.[18]

Under what conditions, however, does separatism become schismatic? This is a vital issue which any contemporary separatist must thoroughly ponder. Three things, it appears, distinguish the schismatic from the separatist.

In the first place, the schismatic believes that his church and his church exclusively deserves to be called the church of Jesus Christ. And as a rule he believes this with heated dogmatism! He disfranchises all denominations and sects but his own; he holds that people who belong to any other fellowship are at best second-class citizens in the Kingdom of God, if in fact they belong to that kingdom. But this has not been the mainstream of our evangelical witness. No, the mainstream flows through a document like the Second London Confession of 1677, one of the most influential and important of the symbols formulated by my own Baptist forebears.

Although we do differ from our brethren who are Paedobaptists in the subject and administration of Baptisme, and such other circumstances as have a necessary dependence on our observance of that Ordinance, and do frequent our own assemblies for our mutual edification, and discharge of those duties, and services which we owe unto God, and in his fear, to each other; yet we would not be from hence misconstrued, as if the discharge of our own consciences herein, did anywayes disoblige or alienate our affections, or conversations from any others that fear the Lord, but that may and do, as we have opportunity participate of the labours of those, whom God hath imbued with abilities above ourselves, and qualified and called to the Ministry of the Word, earnestly desiring to approve ourselves to be such, as follow after peace with holyness, and therefore we alwaies keep that blessed *Irenicum,* or healing Word of the Apostle before our eyes.[19]

There in memorable language flows the mainstream of our evangelical witness, for what is true of Baptists has been true of other fellowships outside the orbit of those larger Protestant communions which emerged after the Reformation. Separatists eschew the schismatic exclusivism which contends that some one fellowship

is the only true church of Jesus Christ. Most illuminating, for example, is the letter which that outstanding leader of the so-called
Plymouth Brethren, Anthony Morris Groves, sent to his much more
rigid colleague, John Nelson Darby:

> The transition your little bodies have undergone, in no longer
> standing for the witness for the glorious and simple *truth,* so much
> as standing forth witnesses against all that they judge error, have
> lowered them in my apprehension from heaven to earth. . . . What
> I mean is, that then, all our thoughts were conversant about how we
> might *ourselves* most effectually manifest forth that life we have
> received by Jesus (knowing that that alone could be as the Shep-
> herd's voice to the living children) and where we might find that
> life in others; and when we were persuaded we had found it, bid-
> ding them, on the Divine claim of this common life (whether their
> thoughts on other matters were narrow or enlarged) to come and
> share with us, in the fellowship of the common Spirit, in the worship
> of our common Head; and as Christ had received them, so would
> we to the glory of God the Father; and farther, that we were free,
> within the limits of truth, to share with them in *part,* though we
> could not in *all,* their services. . . . *I would infinitely rather bear
> with all their evils,* than *separate* from *their good* . . . feeling assured
> in my own heart, that your enlarged and generous spirit, so richly
> taught of the Lord, will one day burst again those bands, which
> narrower minds than yours have encircled you with, and come forth
> again, rather anxious to advance all the living members of the living
> Head into the stature of men, than to be encircled by any little
> bodies, however numerous, that own you for their founder. . . .[20]

Groves in that letter speaks as a separatist who recognizes the
omnipresent hazard of schism; he speaks as a separatist who refuses
to disfranchise all denominations and sects but his own.

For a second thing, the schismatic teaches that every doctrine
of Scripture is equally fundamental. He refuses to recognize any
difference between essentials and non-essentials; everything in the
Bible, he insists, must be put on a level of flat equality. Why not?
Since everything in the Bible is equally true, everything in the Bible,
he argues, must be equally significant. The fact that Paul left a
cloak at Troas is as vital as the fact that Jesus Christ shed His blood
as an atonement for our sins. The schismatic, in short, refuses to
admit the distinction which according to that remarkable French
Calvinist, Auguste LeCerf, keeps Biblical separatism from lapsing
into unbiblical sectarianism. In his *Introduction to Reformed Dogmatics,* LeCerf grapples with a central problem: How do you syn-

thesize church authority and individual liberty? The only viable solution, he argues, rests upon

> the famous distinction, proposed by Calvin, between the articles of faith which constitute the sum of Christianity and those which have not sufficient importance to justify a rupture of external communion. This distinction, which common sense itself demands, is made already in Scripture, here the Apostle compares theological systems to constructions of gold, silver, precious stones, wood, hay and straw, erected on the foundation apart from which nothing can be built, namely, Jesus Christ (I Corinthians 3:10-15). He declares that even those who have erected structures made of fragile and perishable materials "shall be saved, yet so as by fire," providing that they have built upon a solid foundation. The same distinction is made in the Epistle to the Hebrews (6:1). According to these Scriptures, one may speak of fundamental articles of faith, meaning those which it is necessary to believe in order to be saved. Or, again, meaning those which must be professed explicitly by a religious community in order that it may have a right to be considered a living branch of the true Church. In this sense, we may say that the fundamental articles are those which rightly interpret the Gospel, as summarized in the words: "God so loved the world that He gave His only begotten Son, that whosoever believeth in Him should not perish, but have everlasting life" (John 3:16) . . . The definition of fundamental points that we have endeavoured to make enables us to determine, with a sufficiently scientific strictness, where is the visible Church. It does not permit us to delimit the frontiers of the invisible Church, of the mystical society composed of true Christians. Concerning this latter, one cannot say, indicating with the finger: the Church is not here, or the Church is not there. One cannot say this, because the Holy Spirit does not withhold His interior action, nor does Christ withdraw His real presence, at the precise point which a scientifically and logically fundamental formula seem to suggest.[21]

Having shown why this distinction is absolutely necessary, LeCerf proceeds to point out that some biblicists unfortunately degenerate into schismatics precisely because they are not sufficiently biblical!

> We frankly admit that sectarian Biblicism leads inevitably to endless divisions. Since its true name is Legion, like the spirit of the Gadarene demoniac, it is in direct opposition to the prayer of Christ for his disciples: "that they may be one even as we are" (John 17:22). By this fact, it stands condemned on the very battlefield which it has chosen, namely, Scripture. Sects, says the Apostle, are the fruit of a carnal spirit. . . . This is the condemnation of the narrow and legalistic Biblicism which characterized many of the Anglo-Saxon sects of the 18th and 19th centuries. The severe judgment that we have passed on sects must not be interpreted as im-

plying their exclusion from the universal Church, nor even from historic Protestantism. That which is carnal, and even demoniac, in them, must not make us forget that, in other respects, however irregular their methods, they work for the conquest of souls by Jesus Christ. The majority of them firmly maintain the fundamental articles of the Christian faith, rejecting their formulation and ecclesiastical terminology only that they may cling to them with greater tenacity; moreover, as a rule, they are strongly attached to the essential doctrines of the Reformation. Even when they anathematize the Church, the latter must not cease to place the ideal unity of the mystical body of Christ above the narrowness and inconsistencies of certain of its living members. . . . From what has been said it will be seen that we were right in maintaining that the Protestant sects and the ecclesiastical divisions of Reformed Christianity do not necessarily proceed from a faithful and intelligent application of the formal principle of the authority of Scripture. More often than not, they spring from lack of a sense of proportion, which leads men to raise to the rank of an *articulus stantis vel cadentis ecclesiae,* of a dogma necessary to the very existence of the Church, some exegetical interpretation having no vital quality at all.[22]

The separatist who ignores this distinction between essentials and nonessentials degenerates inevitably into a schismatic. Of course! Any Christian who elevates a mere detail of Scripture into a major dogma of faith, insisting that belief in the detail is as necessary as belief in the dogma, passes from the ranks of separatism into the guerilla bands of schism.

In the third place, the schismatic is unconcerned about and indifferent to the tragedy of Christian disunity. Because he considers his own sect the one true church, the sole true church, he holds aloof from all other believers, viewing them with lordly disdain, unconcealed contempt, and downright ill-will. Any fellow-believer who makes an effort to promote evangelical ecumenicity, the schismatic is likely to denounce as an agent of satanic darkness. The welfare of God's global family does not burden him, provided only his little fellowship is walled in securely against enemies. The separatist, on the contrary, grieves over the disunity of God's people. He deplores the scandal of a splintered Christianity. He prays that unity in truth may be achieved. He wishes with all his heart that disciples of the same Lord were indeed "one in hope and doctrine, one in charity."

His ministry basically is not a ministry of divisiveness; it is a ministry of reconciliation. This, then, is what distinguishes the separatist from the schismatic: the separatist is concerned about and burdened by the tragedy of Christian disunity, even though he realizes that, because of persisting sin among Christians, the Church will continue in its multiformity until the end of history. Nevertheless, he heartily endorses LeCerf's irenic statement: "Particular Churches, attached to the same fundamental articles of faith, preaching the same Gospel, having the same ministry, the same sacraments, and communicating in the memory of the same fathers, always leave the door open to possibilities of reconciliation, of federation, and of fruitful collaboration."[23]

So, while repudiating the schismatic spirit, the separatist endorses the judicious appraisal of that compassionate student of schism, S. L. Greenslade:

> Does it follow from the preponderance of evil that all schisms were wrong, that none should ever have occurred? In the absolute sense yes, just as war is in itself evil and should never happen. But were they all wrong in their circumstances? If it is more necessary to-day to emphasize the scandal of disunity, it is also proper to remember that many historic schisms occurred in heartrending circumstances and have borne good as well as evil fruit. First, while it is true that churches in separation from each other may and do lose wholeness and accentuate peculiarities, they may and do develop their own strength. . . . There is much in the total Christian heritage which was not, or was but little, developed in "undivided Christendom," but has been worked out by individual denominations precisely because they were upholding a particular principle or insight over against other groups. . . . Secondly, schisms have preserved liberty. Probably they have seldom done justice to the principle of authority, and many disputes might have been settled, even by weak and fallible humanity, without breach of unity. Still, liberty is a positive value which has so often been threatened by undue circumstances necessary and right. . . . It may therefore be argued — though there will always be some to deny it — that schism has not only preserved the principle of liberty and conscience, and by persistence won back the virtue of tolerance which the early Church first demanded and then betrayed, but also, in some cases, has maintained the truth itself.[24]

Meanwhile, oppressed by his own infirmities, the separatist struggles to live under the authority of God's Word; he struggles to keep separation from degenerating into schism; he struggles to promote unity, charity — and purity! Imperfectly he bears his witness, but he bears it as best he is able, convinced that separatism is not alone an act of obedience to his Saviour and Master but likewise the essential corrective of an errant Christendom.

Chapter Three

A FAITH THAT DOES NOT COMPROMISE
Arnold T. Olson

There were giants in the earth in those days.
(Genesis 6:4)

A school teacher in New York took the members of his class to the Museum of Natural History. One lad became so fascinated with the reproductions of the giant dinosaurs that he stayed behind as the class moved on to other exhibits. Eventually the teacher missed the boy and, retracing his steps, found him still staring at the giants of the past.

"They must have been big and strong," said the lad.

"Yes," replied the teacher, "they were strong."

"But there are none living today," continued the boy.

"No," his teacher answered, "they are extinct."

"Why is it," asked the boy, "that the biggest and strongest animals are gone, but the fleas, the flies, and the mosquitoes are still here?"

The teacher, who was supposed to know all the answers, was ready for this question. He went on to explain that ages ago there was a change of climate in the world. The ice age moved in and destroyed the giants.

As one studies the history of the church one must conclude that there were giants in the earth in those days — intellectual and spiritual giants who courageously and skillfully met the enemies of our faith. The question naturally arises, "Are we producing spiritual giants today?"

Is it not true that there has been a change of climate and that an ice age has moved in upon us? Instead of the church producing giants it, with all of its efforts, can do no more than create inept sparring partners who waste their time fighting shadows. Instead of saints who know God through the blessed Book and who prevail in prayer we are now producing puny, anemic church members.

40

The giants of the early church knew who the enemy was and where the pitfalls to our faith were located. Each of the great councils was called to meet a threat against the faith.

The Apostolic Creed, the Nicene or Creed of Chalcedon, and the Athanasian Creed were written to meet the threats against the faith. These were all results of lengthy struggles and symbols of victories over the enemies of the faith from without and within. They stood as bulwarks against the infiltration of pagan philosophies. Christianity had to take a positive position. The forces seeking intentionally or unintentionally to suffocate Christianity would have succeeded had it not been for the uncompromising position and positive expressions of the early saints.

It has been well said that "a journey of a thousand miles begins with a single step." The journey of two thousand years began when the church fathers recognized the real enemies of the faith and took on these foes in a life-or-death struggle. Each of the early creeds came into existence in direct reply to some specific philosophy which, if it had gone unchallenged, would have eventually leavened the whole loaf. Many of these philosophies are back with us and — worse yet — within the organized church. Making up a fifth column within, they are simply waiting for the four columns of ecumenism, communism, secularism and paganism to make their final approach from without.

The early summaries of our faith were primarily a defense of the Gospel against the heresies from without, especially as they related to the Person of Christ. These were not lengthy and complicated summaries of theology written in cloistered studies, but in command posts on the fields of conflict. They were produced by dedicated men in the darkest hours when the truth of the Scriptures, which they loved more than life itself, was being perverted.

As time went on, however, tradition was added as being on par with the Scriptures and thus came the Reformation. Unfortunately, however, the Reformation, though making a return to the basic doctrines of the early church, also led to a series of conflicts between sincere, dedicated but powerful personalities. From then until comparatively recent times the new creeds were primarily the reflections of disagreements within the church. Theologian rose up against theologian, believer against believer. Non-essentials became matters of primary importance. The statements of faith became more and more complicated, increasingly divisive, less and less inspiring.

It was not until the latter half of the last century that history notes a return to the simple and uniting summaries of our faith. Groups began to join in recognition of a common foe. The fundamentals of our faith once more became the common denominator for many denominational groups as well as independent missionary fellowships. Interdenominational Bible institutes sprang up to meet the hunger for more knowledge about and from the Book.

This very Church in which we are assembled, for example — the First Baptist Church of Minneapolis — became the meeting place for fundamentalists from this entire area who united against the forces of modernism. Great crowds assembled. It was a climate producing spiritual giants. The distinctives of evangelicalism were clear. There were revivals in many churches throughout the midwest.

But again the climate changed. Leaders turned their backs upon the common enemy and began to fight one another. The Arminian fought the Calvinist; the pre-tribulationist would have no dealings with the post-tribulationist; the one who claimed a second blessing felt out of place with the one still enjoying only his first blessing and with the one going on to a third and a fourth. The fundamentalist conventions became part of history. The giants began to disappear from the scene while little men with limited visions moved in to take pot-shots at one another.

An editorial in the *Sunday School Times* summarizes the situation:

> There must, of course, be a proper, vigorous concern for the preservation and promulgation of true biblical faith today. We cannot allow unbelief to go unchallenged. But have we who profess to love and serve the Lord Jesus Christ not gone too far in our eagerness to preserve and defend orthodoxy? Have we not raised some false tests of orthodoxy, such as whether you cooperate in a Billy Graham crusade or not; what version of the Bible you read; what view of the rapture you take; what denomination or what church council you belong to; what speakers you go to hear or what writers you quote; and what you think about Communism's threat and how to meet it?
>
> As a matter of fact, none of these things determines whether a person is a Bible-believing, born-again Christian. These are false tests of orthodoxy. And it is the efforts of those who would classify

people on the basis of such tests as these that are so damaging to the real unity all evangelicals, conservatives and fundamentalists so desperately need today.

When the attack of scientific, evolutionary liberalism came against true biblical faith, there was united action against it that cut across the differences on such matters as baptism, the Lord's Supper, eternal security, election, and church government. These were important differences, compared to the false tests of orthodoxy raised today, and yet for the sake of opposing liberalism and secularism the early fundamentalists allowed liberty on these matters. This was the strength of the fundamentalist movement; it united Anglicans, Baptists, Presbyterians, Lutherans, Methodists, and others, because of agreement on a common core of doctrinal essentials, such as the inspiration and authority of the Bible; the substitutionary, blood atonement of Christ; the necessity of repentance and faith for salvation; the virgin birth and the bodily resurrection of Christ, and the hope of His personal return to earth.[1]

There is plenty of opposition to compromise among evangelicals today. Our trouble is not so much over the question of compromise but a definition of evangelical faith.

I doubt that in our generation we shall solve the problem of the diversity of denominations or the difference in church polity, the ordinances, and the minor differences in theology. Nor am I so sure that this is desirable. In spite of the attacks made against us, let us not lose sight of the fact that the purity of the church is just as important as the unity of the church. God has blessed these many groups through the centuries. "The wisdom that is from above is *first pure,* then peaceable" (James 3:17).

However, if we are to enjoy unity without necessarily experiencing union — and remember it is possible to have union without unity, and vice versa — we must prepare a new declaration of evangelical distinctives. We must prepare a statement which, like the creeds of old, summarizes our faith in the face of neo-orthodoxy and ecumenism. We need to rediscover the real meaning of the church, the true basis of Christian unity. I have been wondering if we shouldn't also take a second look at the ecumenical movement in the light of the Scriptures. It may be that in so doing some of us will have to retract articles and even books we have written in defense of an evangelical ecumenism.

What are the basic principles of an evangelical faith? What are the things commonly believed among us in spite of those minor differences? Where do we draw the line? Where do we say, "In these there can be no compromise"?

It seems to me that there are three points on which there can be no compromise. They can be summarized in three words — the Scriptures, the experience and the expectation.

I. *The Scriptures*

The true evangelical not only considers the Bible as the source of knowledge, but the supreme court from which there is no appeal — the final authority in all matters of faith and practice. In this there can be no compromise. The authority of the Bible is the keystone of the evangelical faith. Evangelicals through the centuries have believed that the Holy Bible is the Word of God.

Up until about two hundred years ago the authority of the Bible as being — not just containing — the Word of God was accepted by almost every branch of Christendom. Protestants and Roman Catholics agree to this. The difference lies in the fact that Rome holds to the belief that the church has the exclusive and final right to the interpretation of the Scriptures. Even at the time of the Reformation there was no dispute over the authority of the Bible. It was rather over the authority of the church. The Roman Catholic Church has not changed its position on the authority of the church since the Council of Trent in 1545, and evangelical Christianity has clung to the authority of the Scriptures.

Evangelicals of today owe a debt to the Reformation on this point. It was this return to the Bible and the Bible only as the authoritative source of divine revelation that gave power to the church and caused its reform and revival. A climate conducive to revival and the production of spiritual giants is contemporaneous with such a faith in the Scriptures. It might be well to remind ourselves that this evangelical distinctive is not the exclusive heritage of any particular group. J. Marcellus Kik summarizes some of the great declarations in his book, *Ecumenism and the Evangelicals*.[2]

The Lutheran Formula of Concord (1576) states, "We believe, confess, and teach that the only rule and norm, according to which all dogmas and all doctrines ought to be esteemed and judged, is no other whatever than the prophetic and apostolic writings both of the Old and New Testament."

The French Confession (1559) attests, "No authority, whether of antiquity, or custom, or numbers, or edicts, or decrees, or councils, or visions, or miracles, should be opposed to these Holy Scriptures, but on the contrary, all things should be examined, regulated, and reformed according to them."

The Belgic Confession (1561) declares, "We believe that these Holy Scriptures fully contain the will of God . . . we reject with all our hearts whatsoever doth not agree with this infallible rule."

The 39 Articles of the Church of England (1562) contain this statement, "The Holy Scriptures containeth all things necessary to salvation: so that whatsoever is not read therein, nor may be proved therein, nor may be proved thereby, is not required of any man, that it should be believed as an article of faith."

The Westminster Confession of Faith (1647) says, ". . . therefore it pleased the Lord, at sundry times and in divers manners, to reveal Himself, to declare His will unto His church; and afterwards, for the better preserving and propagating of the truth, and for the sure establishment and comfort of the Church against the corruption of the flesh, and the malice of Satan and of the World, to commit the same wholly unto writing; which maketh the Holy Scriptures to be most necessary; those former ways of God revealing His will unto His people being now ceased."

The New Hampshire Baptist Confession (1833) testifies, "We believe the Holy Bible . . . has God for its author, salvation for its ends, and truth without any mixture of error for its matter; that it reveals the principle by which God will judge us; and therefore is and shall remain to the end of the world, the true center of Christian union, the supreme standard by which all human conduct, creeds, opinions should be tried."

Other declarations could be cited to show that the full and final authority of the Scriptures was accepted by all of the historic denominations. So far as is known no one has officially changed such a declaration of faith, but many attempts have been made to modify, revise, or eliminate such a firm affirmation in interpretation, though not necessarily in the letter.

The last century, however, has brought a change. Divisions have developed, schisms have taken place, unity has been disturbed by those who have sought to lead the church away from this position. They have done a real disservice to Christian unity by attempting to undermine faith in the Scriptures. Many of us who are classified as members of sects and looked upon as standing on the periphery of the historic church were forced there by those within the church who would cast doubt on the veracity of the Scriptures.

Many in these movements today noted a lack of authority in the historic denominations. Others who have remained and are trying nobly and courageously to correct the situation — May God bless them! — are quarantined. Unless they win the battle there is little hope that the church will find true unity.

In this change of climate we have gone through two periods. The first was when the modernists sought to discredit the Bible. They engaged in an all-out attack against the doctrine that the Bible is the inerrant Word of God. The frontal attack reached its peak at the turn of the century and continued through the 1920's. It was against this enemy that fundamentalism directed its defense.

The experiences and lessons of World War II, however, put modernism to rout. Evangelicalism's greatest threat no longer comes from that area. To fight the so-called modernists is to fight shadows — to waste ammunition on an imaginary enemy. The effort to destroy faith in the full and final authority of the Bible now takes on a more subtle form. It has many names, the most familiar being neo-orthodoxy and neo-liberalism. This movement has restored the Bible to a position of respect, but still does not admit its authority. It is summarized in an article by John A. Witmer:

> Dialectical theology did restore the Bible to a position of honor in Christian thought as "'a sign-post to Revelation," an instrument or record or vehicle to witness that could become the Word of God as God used it in the revelatory encounter with man. The Bible was considered unique among religious books, "the indispensable witness" to the revelation of God in Christ. Both in the public ministry of the churches and in individual Christian experience the Bible once again began to be seriously studied and used.
>
> Bible-believing Christians can rejoice in these positive results from neo-orthodoxy's "rediscovery of the Bible," but dangers exist as well. The naturalistic biblical criticism that spawned modernism is accepted by neo-orthodoxy with little or no change. The Genesis records of creation, the Fall and the Flood are called myths. The patriarchs are not historical characters; in fact, historical and scientific reliability throughout the Bible is denied. Prophecy and miracles are suspect and rationalistically explained. In essence the

Bible remains a human book which God designs to use because it witnesses to and interprets revelatory encounters. In its view of the Bible neo-orthodoxy merely spreads supernaturalistic veneer over the naturalistic position of modernism. Van Til's picture of neo-orthodoxy as a massive complex of air castles with no foundation is graphically correct.

The influence of neo-orthodoxy in the full spectrum of its views — itself an evidence of basic subjectivity and relativism — remains powerful in the Christian world today. But reactions to it have produced other forces allied with it in opposition to the historic Church doctrine of the Bible. Modernism in sackcloth and ashes has repented and has adjusted its position to deal more realistically with the Bible. The new face of modernism is called neo-liberalism, and it has already supplanted neo-orthodoxy as the theological fashion in many of the old strongholds of modernism. Neo-liberals, in DeWolf's words, recognize that "the Bible itself is not the pure Word of God." As a result, when reading the Bible you must "discriminate between the word of God and the words of men." Neo-liberals lead, of course, in "this first-hand serious discriminating search for the true word of God through the words of the Bible."[3]

It is here that evangelicals must cling to a faith that does not compromise. J. Marcellus Kik draws attention to the importance of this point:

Ecumenism will never in a thousand and one years achieve the goal of Christian unity until it settles the question of authority. Has God revealed the way, the truth, and the life for ecumenism in the written Word or is human experience authoritative? Is Christianity the revealed religion? Sooner or later ecumenism must grapple with the question of authority even as it is struggling with the nature of the church. As long as everyone has an authority, a confession, a Lord, a Christ, a Church, we despair of the realization of unity.

Evangelicals have settled the question of authority. They build the faith, their creeds, their churches upon the foundation of the apostles and prophets, Christ Jesus Himself being the chief cornerstone. They strive to be apostolic in doctrine. They subordinate human creeds to Scripture. While it is true that some regard their particular creeds as thoroughly agreeable to the Scriptures, nevertheless, they maintain the principle that the inscripturated Word is the final authority for faith and life and that human creeds must constantly be judged by the Scriptures. This is because evangelicals have found the common source for their creeds in the Bible that they can say in sincerity and truth that their agreements are far greater than their disagreements. On vital doctrines they do not have to "agree to disagree." The creeds of historic denominations show wonderful accord on the authority of the Scriptures, Trinity, creation, the fall of man, deity of Christ, justification, saving faith, the last judgment, heaven and hell, and the second coming of the Lord.[4]

II. *Personal Experience*

Evangelicals may differ as to the place of election, emotion, external exercise in the conversion of a soul, but they are united in believing that a personal and vital experience produced by the Holy Spirit is the only beginning of a Christian life. There may be a variety of experiences. There may be differences as to the degree in which outward exercises and the ordinances assist in transformation, but all agree that a regeneration is essential. This is why we are able to work together in cooperative efforts to evangelize. It is also the place where evangelicals and liberals part company when attempts are made to cooperate in evangelism.

An evangelical must not only contend for the faith — he must preach the new birth and continue to cry, "Ye must be born again," even in a society which prides itself on sophistication.

There is a common faith. There is also a common salvation. The Epistle of Jude warns against those who would compromise this salvation: "Beloved, when I gave all diligence to write unto you of the common salvation, it was needful for me to write unto you, and exhort you that ye should earnestly contend for the faith which was once delivered unto the saints" (Jude 3).

Once we deny the authority of the Bible, the next step is easy. We elevate man to a place where he needs no Saviour and where he has within himself the capabilities of saving his own soul, transforming his own life, and determining his own destiny.

This experience has its objective as well as its subjective side. Evangelicals must take care lest we lose sight of the one in our emphasis on the other. There must be the experience of the new birth but only through a personal faith in Jesus Christ, and that brings us back to our first distinctive — the authority of the Scriptures for it is here we find who Jesus is. It must be the Christ of the Word — only He can transform lives, not the human Christ, the mythical Christ, the synthetic Christ, the metamorphased Christ, but the Christ as revealed not by flesh and blood but by the Scriptures.

The early evangelicals recognized the importance of this. The ecumenical creeds of the first centuries were written to declare the truth as the person of Christ. They believed that there was salvation in none other than the Christ, the Son of the living God. This faith in the person of Christ as revealed in the Scriptures is the very essence of Christianity. The reformers, returning to the first principles, rightly considered the doctrine of justification by faith as essential to evangelical Christianity and any denial of or deviation from that truth as fatal to the very existence of the church.

Church membership no longer calls for such a faith, an experience of conversion, or a personal witness to Christ as Saviour. The extent of this departure from the evangelical position is evident in a statement I read recently in a church bulletin. It said: "Why not unite with our church? This church respects the right of everyone to think for himself. We have no dogma and no creed. We are only trying to make a better world."

W. Curry Mavis insists that spiritual regeneration is the very genius of evangelical Christianity. In his book, *Beyond Conformity*, he states:

> There are many in contemporary Christianity who believe that such alleged changes in life are fantastic. There are multitudes of modern church people who are as incredulous about genuine spiritual rebirth as was Nicodemus. On the other hand, evangelicals believe that definite and decisive spiritual renewals are necessary. They are more than a theory and more than a doctrine. They are basic to Christian living. Evangelicals believe that man cannot live the Christian life without a positive, spiritual regeneration. . . .
>
> Moreover, evangelicals believe that it is necessary to have personally transformed persons so that others may be saved. The "once born" may build up an ecclesiastical institution but it takes the "twice born" to build a spiritual kingdom. . . .
>
> A conversion experience that has the elements of assurance, of forgiveness of sins and spiritual regeneration is an experience of depth. This is the genius of the Christian religion.[5]

This evangelical distinctive is also the evangelical's answer to the charge that we are blind to most current social problems and inept at solving those we do see. History refutes this. The great evangelical revivals resulted in social revolutions. The giants of evangelicalism were instrumental in bringing about social reforms in the last century. However, to use the thesis of Dr. Mavis, "The genius of the evangelical method of redeeming society is seen in the personal redemption of individuals. The social philosophy of evangelicals in relation to social reconstruction, inasmuch as it is articulate, is that society can be changed through changed individuals."[6]

This is part of the evangelical's faith in which there can be no compromise. To fail here would be to fail utterly.

Recently Professor Osmo Tiilila of the University of Helsinki broke with the national church and resigned from the ordained ministry in a protest against modern trends which are leading the church away from its central purpose. In his statement he criticized the new methods of church work aimed at reaching an understanding of modern man without primarily seeking his conversion from sin. He said he wanted to stress that the "greatest danger to the church is the neglect of the message of eternal life."

III. The Expectation

Since the first days of the Christian church evangelicals have been looking for that "blessed hope and glorious appearing of the great God and our Saviour, Jesus Christ."

We may differ as to the pre-tribulation and post-tribulation rapture, the pre- and post-millennial coming, but we are agreed that the final solution to the problems of this world are in the hands of the King of Kings who will someday make the kingdoms of this world His very own.

At times in history the flame of hope has been burning brightly in the darkness of persecutions. At other times the entire church has been asleep, but asleep while waiting. Nevertheless, evangelicals look for a personal return of Christ.

The evil servant said in his heart, "My Lord delayeth his coming." He did not reject the fact of His coming, but postponed the time of His return. He missed the sense of urgency and the purifying power of the hope. This resulted first in a smiting of his fellow servants and, eventually, association with the enemy.

Have not evangelicals followed a somewhat similar pattern? We are agreed that Christ's return is on the calendar, but have proceeded to attack fellow servants during the waiting period. While not denying the fact of His coming, we have often missed the force of this truth. Some have even been found in the very camp of the enemy.

Those who compromise regarding the Second Coming of Christ

have first rejected the authority of the Bible and then man's need of regeneration. The natural result is the conclusion that man, capable of solving his own problems, can through his knowledge of science bring in the kingdom. If there is any second coming it is spiritual — neither visible nor personal.

To the early church the coming of the Lord was always "at hand." Though some may argue that certain views on eschatology are of more recent origin, it cannot be denied that the historic creeds stated clearly that the personal return of Christ offered the only final solutions to the problems of peace and universal justice.

These, then, are the basic truths commonly believed among evangelicals. This is a faith that must not be compromised. But in standing true to these convictions, we must stand together. How tragic that we should permit the differences — the minors — to become majors in our dealings with one another. Sincere theologians have disagreed through the centuries. Can we reconcile these differences in a conference or even in a single generation? Remember, too, that the blessings of God have been on many movements which may have held to certain principles and practices which you cannot accept.

We thank God for the great declarations of principles set down by Calvin and his followers. The history of the influence of Calvinism, especially outside Geneva, is a glorious one, but the followers of Arminius, such as in Methodism and the modern Pentecostal and Nazarene movements, have also been blessed and used of God. The great state church movements of Europe preserved the truth through trying years, but the Free Churches brought the message of salvation to many souls even within the church. God blessed the Congregationalists in their opposition to the Church of England and used the dissenter group to found this nation, and its principles of church polity became the basis for the political policies of the country.

We thank God for Martin Luther and the other reformers. One wonders where we might be today apart from the Reformation, but remember that the anabaptists, so persecuted by the reformers, led the way in the great pietistic revivals and missionary movements. Evangelicals who hold to the doctrine of baptism for believers only and that by immersion should bear in mind that the Reformation movements — Lutherans, Calvinists, Arminians — held to infant baptism.

God has blessed all who believed the Bible to be the full and final authority, who preached regeneration by the Holy Spirit through a personal faith in Jesus Christ, who looked for Christ's personal return regardless of their views on baptism, election, apostolic succession, and details of eschatology; but God has not prospered spiritually those who have discredited the Book, belittled experience, and denied Christ's return regardless of how right they were in other matters!

We find it easy to criticize the schisms of the past. Many of us are part of movements we did not start and others remain in movements with which they cannot wholly agree. This, however, is our hour. Cannot we agree that these are the great distinctives of our common faith? Can we not respect one another's sincerity, intelligence and scholarship in other matters over which we may differ? Can we not here covenant to take the offensive even to storming the gates of hell in this faith and that we shall not compromise this faith no matter what the trends may be around us?

Ours is a common heritage. Let us then say with John Wesley, "If thy heart be as my heart, give me thy hand."

Chapter Four

CHRISTIAN UNITY IN HISTORICAL PERSPECTIVE

Earle E. Cairns

While any thinking Christian is sympathetic to the ideal of Christian unity, he may be pardoned for having a desire to examine the cry for ecumenical cooperation from an historical perspective in order to see what light history — as well as Scripture — might throw on this subject.

Evangelicals have a right to raise questions concerning the nature of the unity Christ prayed for in John 17, the broad inclusivism of the ecumenical movement with its weak doctrinal statement, the danger of a world church which seems to be the goal of some ecumenical enthusiasts, and the danger that the ecumenical movement might become a social, economic and political force to the detriment of its spiritual mission.

The interest of many evangelicals in Biblical prophecy makes them wary of international ecclesiastical organizations which unwittingly may pave the way for the integrating force of antichrist who will coordinate ecclesiastical as well as political and economic life under his absolute control.

These divergent viewpoints suggest the need for an historical examination of what Christians have thought and done about Christian unity during the history of the church. Examination of the historical data suggests that unity has been achieved by the *expulsion* of those who were judged heretical by Biblical and creedal standards, by *coercion* in a universal or state church, and — in modern times — by *voluntary* action.

I. Unity by Expulsion, from the Old Catholic Church to 380 A.D.

In the second century problems of schism and heresy confronted the New Testament church which threatened both its structural and doctrinal unity. Shortly before A.D. 100, Clement of Rome addressed himself to the schism in the church at Corinth in his Epistle to the Corinthians.

Some officials of the church had evidently been deprived of their rightful offices in the church by a schismatic group.[1] This was a serious matter in Clement's opinion because bishops or elders were in a line of apostolic succession from the apostles who had received their authority from Christ. These elders or bishops were to be the guarantors of the oral teachings and the Gospel of Christ and the apostles. This would keep the church doctrinally sound until the completion of the canon by the consensus of the church under guidance of the Holy Spirit. He develops his argument in chapters 42-44 of his letter in an effort to end the dissension and schism in the Corinthian church. Schism was not to be allowed to mar the unity of the church.

Ignatius, bishop of Antioch who was martyred for his faith, wrote several letters to churches in Asia shortly after the beginning of the second century. In these letters the transition from the twofold order of bishops or elders and deacons of Clement to the threefold order of bishops, elders or presbyters and deacons is clearly set forth. He is our first major witness to the rise of the bishop as distinct from the presbyter or elder. Congregations are to be in harmony with the deacons, presbyters and bishops who through apostolic succession are in harmony with Christ. This will create a blameless unity which will make them "partakers of God always."[2]

He believes that apart from these democratically selected and divinely appointed men who witness to Christ there can be no catholic (universal) church.[3] Schismatics would not inherit the kingdom of God.[4] His exhortations were not given to justify a hierarchy as an end, but to insist that this heirarchy in direct line of apostolic succession from Christ and the apostles preserved the oral teachings of Christ. This alone would prevent the rise of heresies, such as the docetic heresy, which is mentioned in several of his letters. This heresy denied the essential humanity of Christ by making Him a phantom.[5]

Irenaeus, the opponent of the gnostic heresy, also emphasized the importance of obedience to the bishops because they are the holders of the oral Gospel which came from Christ through the apostles.[6] Tertullian asserted that doctrine which accords with that of the apostolic churches is truth which comes from the apostles who received it from Christ.[7] Because of this belief both Irenaeus and Tertullian drew up rules of faith based on the Scriptures which were the earliest written statements of the doctrine of the early church.

These and other fathers of the early church thus made apostolic doctrine an important consideration in granting fellowship. Heretical gnostics, according to Irenaeus, had no place in the church, and Tertullian was just as adamant in his opposition to Praxeas the Monarchian. Any view which depreciated the person or work of Christ was not admissible, and such persons were to be judged as heretics for whom the church had no room.

The bishop was the bond to unite them in a unity which accepted the oral and later written rules of faith derived from the Bible. Unity was to be in the faith or truth as well as love, and heretics were to be excluded from the fellowship of which they were unworthy. Unity was to be achieved by expulsion from the church of unworthy persons and parties who dared to deny the faith or promoted schism. This discipline was within the church, a voluntary union of Christians.

The Roman state entered the picture in the period between 325 and 451, urging the church to unity when doctrinal divisions arose. This would, by making the church one in doctrine and practice, create a unity of the church which would enable it to be the cement of society, the function which Constantine felt it should fulfill. The Donatist schism over the ones who had given up the Scriptures in the persecution under Diocletian was resolved in an ecumenical council at Arles in 314. Constantine even presided at the Council of Nicaea in 325 and worked to bring about doctrinal unity.

Later councils were called to deal with the relation of the two natures in Christ and the problem of the nature of man's disability which was created by the dispute between Augustine and Pelagius over the nature of original sin. In all of these state-supported endeavors to maintain the unity of the church it will be seen that the unity was one based upon correct doctrine with no idea of compromising the truth. The absolute truth of the canon was to be expressed in relative creeds which were to be the touchstone of unity. Membership in the church was still a voluntary matter, but exclusion was the lot of those who could not accept the doctrinal unity of the faith.

II. Unity by Coercion, 380-1648

From 380 until the Reformation in 1517 the universal state or a universal church supported by temporal authorities demanded unity of all Christians. To unity by expulsion from the church was added unity by compulsion.

The voluntary association of oneself with the church gave way to birth into the *universal* church and compulsory allegiance on pain both of spiritual and temporal penalties. The bishop of Rome claimed to be the supreme bishop to whom all must give allegiance. Christianity became the state religion of the Roman empire in 380, but at that date the most the bishop of Rome could claim was the primacy accorded to him by Cyprian in his work *Of the Unity of the Catholic Church* and by Canon 3 of the Council of Constantinople in 381. In 445 the Emperor Valentinian accorded to Leo I, bishop of Rome, recognition of him as the supreme bishop. He declared that no church official should act contrary to his will, and that all should obey his enactments. Under the protection of the empire and later with the aid of the Franks, the Roman bishop was able to consolidate his claims to supremacy over Christendom.

Salvation, as a result of historical evolution, developed from being a matter of a personal relationship to Christ by faith to one of admission to a corporate body or institution by a sacramental system. This system—which was essential to salvation—was in the hands of the hierarchy headed by the bishop of Rome. The hierarchy thus had a monopoly on salvation by its control of the sacraments, exclusion from which meant spiritual death.

Under Gregory VII (1073-1085) and Innocent III (1198-1216) the principle of unity by coercion was extended. Gregory VII in his *Dictatus Papae*—which, if he did not write it, expressed his ideology and practice—claimed jurisdiction over all men and institutions. Priest and civil potentate alike were to submit to him on pain of exclusion from the church. The pope was to be the only prince "whose feet are kissed by all princes." He was only temporarily successful in exerting this power over Henry IV, the emperor of the Holy Roman empire.

Although heretics had been excluded from the church from the earliest days, there had been few churches excluded until the decisions of the councils forced out dissenters. Monophysite churches sprang up in Abyssinia, Egypt and Syria and Nestorian churches in Persia between 325 and 451.

Far more serious was the series of quarrels over the date of Easter, the use of images, the western addition of the filioque clause in the Nicene Creed, and other matters which led in 1054 to the separation of the Eastern and Western churches. Several attempts at reunion were unsuccessful.

Even the monolithic western Roman Catholic Church was not free from disunity in its leadership. Between 1378 and 1417 there were two—and for a time, three— popes each claiming to be the Vicar of Christ. Reformers in order to end this "Great Schism" proposed councils which would change the constitution of the church so that future popes would be constitutional rather than absolute monarchs, such as Innocent III had been. While the councils were successful in ending the schism in the headship of the church, they were unsuccessful in making the Roman Catholic Church a constitutional monarchy.

After 1517 the unity of compulsion in a universal church supported by a universal state gave way during the Reformation to unity by compulsion in state or territorial churches into which one was born. These state churches were creedal, and the period from 1517 to 1648 was marked by the formation of many Protestant creeds beginning with the Lutheran Augsburg Confession in 1530. Unity was closely associated with doctrinal formulations in a fashion similar to that of the ecumenical councils of 325 and 451. These Lutheran, Calvinistic and Anglican state church leaders believed that they were in the line of continuity of the church because their reformist policies were to rediscover apostolic and Old Catholic doctrine.

The Anabaptists were the exception because they saw discontinuity between churches of their day and the early church and they wanted a restoration of the faith and practice of the early church instead of mere reformation. They also opposed the link between church and state, insisting upon a pure church of adult baptized believers. Their demands for separation of church and state and religious freedom made them the forerunners in the movement after 1648 which led to religious denominational pluralism.

Even though the rise of national territorial states created Protestant creedal state churches dependent upon national governments for support between 1517 and 1648, the reformers never forgot that there was a holy catholic church which they refused to associate with the visible Roman Catholic Church. They believed in the *communio sanctorum*, the communions of saints, which made them one in spirit though in separate national churches. Luther, Zwingli, Melanchthon, Calvin, Knox, the leading Anglican bishops and later the Baptists and Methodists believed in an invisible catholic church which was manifested by the true preaching of the Word and the right administration of the two Biblical sacraments. Calvin even based the organization of his *Institutes* upon the parts of the Apostles' Creed. Catholic church and communion of saints were synonymous phrases. They were united in rejecting a visible Roman Catholic Church united under a papal monarchy. Their revolt was against this rather than catholicity.

They even stated that they might remain in the Church if it would adopt a conciliar catholicism. This would mean the holding of a representative church council which would cleanse the church of traditional accretions of unscriptural sacramentalism, liturgy and papal dictatorship. Luther, on November 28, 1518, proposed a council which would represent the "holy catholic Church" and be superior to the pope in matters of faith. Calvin also wanted such a council. That the conciliar attempts to contain Protestantism within the church by truly reforming it were not successful was the fault of the papacy which rejected reform.

Even though the Roman Catholic Church rejected reform as the price of unity, the various reformers made attempts to achieve Protestant unity by conciliarism on the basis of the Word and sacraments. They were interested in one catholic church and when attempts at conciliar reform of that church failed, they turned to conciliarism to unite the various groups of Protestants. Although intraconfessional concords were drawn up, doctrinal differences and national churches prevented the successful consummation of Protestant catholicity.

III. From Denominational Pluralism to Ecumenism, 1648-

With the establisment of the principle of toleration for those outside the state church, denominations based on the views of the reformers and their successors emerged.

During the eighteenth century the ecumenical spirit was evidenced in two attempts to reunite Christians. Zinzendorf was a bishop of the Moravian Church which emerged from the United Brethren who found shelter on his estate at Berthelsdorf in Saxony. He tried without success to bring about a union of the Pietist movement and Lutheranism in order to end the differences which separated the faculties of the Universities of Halle and Wittenberg. Halle's vigorous spiritual life and Wittenberg's doctrinal orthodoxy would, he thought, be an excellent union.

When he visited Pennsylvania in 1741 he worked with a Reformed lay preacher, Henry Antes, to unite German Protestants of that state into an evangelical union. Seven synods were called between January and June of 1742 with an average attendance of over 100 Lutheran, Reformed, Mennonite, Quakers, Shwenkfeldians, Moravians and Dunkards at each. Suspicion of Zinzendorf, a titled nobleman of dubious tact, led, however, to failure in this attempt "to make visible the invisible church."

Fear of the appointment of an Anglican bishop in the 13 colonies resulted in 1760 in a proposal in a sermon by Ezra Stiles, a Congregational pastor in Newport, Rhode Island, for a union of Congregational churches. Ultimately he hoped that Presbyterians might be included. Thirty Presbyterian and Congregational ministers met at Elizabethtown, New Jersey, in November, 1766, and worked out a "Plan of Union for the Christian Union." This organization was in effect until 1776 when the Declaration of Independence removed the threat of an Anglican bishop in the colonies.

William Carey in a letter in 1806 to Andrew Fuller, secretary of the Baptist Missionary Society, proposed a meeting at the Cape of Good Hope in 1810 of "all denominations of Christians." This would be followed by a similar meeting every ten years. The Lutherans, John V. Andreae and George Calixtus, the Arminian Hugo Grotius and John Amos Commenius, the great educator of the United Brethren, all made proposals of unity in the seventeenth century. These proposals for various reasons were not successful but testify to the persistence of the desire for unity in the church. All of these men still wanted a minimum creed based on the Bible as the basis for union.

During the nineteenth century the evangelicals in England achieved practical unity with a consensus of doctrine to permit cooperation in social reforms, such as the ending of the slave trade and slavery, better treatment of the insane, workers and the inmates of prisons. They all, whether Low Church Evangelical, Methodist, Presbyterian or Congregationalist, accepted the depravity of man, personal conversion and the authority of the Bible as well as its plenary inspiration. This unity was one of action outside the church in extra-church organizations set up to achieve spiritual and practical goals. Men such as Wesley, Wilberforce, Macaulay and others cooperated to achieve these common humanitarian ends of love which was inspired by their faith.

But the real center of the ecumenical spirit and drive was nineteenth century America. The Great Awakening of the mid-eighteenth century under Frelinghuysen, the Tennents, Jonathan Edwards and George Whitefield; the Second Awakening in the southern and eastern colleges, such as at Yale under Timothy Dwight, and the western camp meetings of McGready helped to develop intercolonial unity. Such moves to ecumenism among the denominations took the forms of cooperation in interdenominational organizations and inter- and intraconfessional organic reunion of denominations and confederation along national and international lines in the nineteenth and twentieth centuries.

The organization of such *interdenominational* groups as the British and Foreign Bible Society in 1804 and the London Sunday School Union of the year before was paralleled in this country by the creation of many interdenominational organizations after 1800. This was a result of revival and the challenge to win the settlers on the frontier by cooperative effort.

Congregationalists and Presbyterians united their efforts to carry on home missions in the Plan of Union of 1801. The American Board of Commissioners for Foreign Missions was set up in 1810 to meet the challenge of Judson and his friends who desired to go out as foreign missionaries. It soon included Presbyterians and Reformed. The American Bible Society was set up in 1816 to provide Bibles and in 1825 the American Tract Society was formed to provide religious reading material for those on the frontier. The American Sunday School Union was created in 1824 to coordinate Sunday school work and to provide materials for use in such schools. Cooperation went still further in the creation of the Temperance Society in 1826. Christians cooperated over denominational lines in all these common endeavors.

Later in the century such organizations as the YMCA (1851), Christian Endeavor (1881), the Student Volunteer Movement (1886) which grew out of a student meeting at Moody's Northfield school, and the World Student Christian Movement (1895) under John R. Mott continued the development of interdenominational cooperation.

The idea of closer association in *confederate organizations* also appealed to nineteenth century American churchmen. Samuel Schmucker, the president of the Lutheran Theological Seminary in Gettysburg wrote in 1838 a small book for interconfessional union titled *Fraternal Appeal to the American Churches* which was circulated by the American Tract Society. In 1846 he wrote "Overture on Christian Union" which was also signed by 41 other ministers of larger Protestant denominations. He asked for mutual recognition, intercommunion and consultation among the denominations united in a world confederate type of church.

These desires found fruition in the organization of the Evangelical Alliance in 1846 in London. It was an international confederate organization, mainly of individuals, based upon an evangelical creed similar to that of the present National Association of Evangelicals. An American branch was founded in 1867 and lasted until its dissolution in 1944. Josiah Strong, its general secretary after 1886, wanted a gospel to change the environment as well as the individual, and the whole man as well as his spirit. Liberal theologians with their interest in social action and doctrinal latitudinarianism found the creed of the Alliance too binding.

Philip Schaff, the great church historian who taught at the Reformed Seminary in Lancaster, Pennsylvania, gave a lecture on "The Reunion of Christendom" to a meeting of religious leaders at the Chicago World's Fair in 1893. He pled for a "federal or confederate" union in which each church would be independent in internal affairs but would recognize its sister churches as equal and cooperate with them in "general enterprises" such as preaching the Gospel, missions, defense of the faith, helping the poor and promoting moral reform. With some modifications this has been the program of modern ecumenism.

With the rise of many institutional churches which sought to meet the needs of the whole man with education, recreation, religion and medical care, the need for cooperation among such churches led to the organization in 1894 of the Open and Institutional Church League. It emphasized social service and interdenominational cooperation. In 1901 a National Federation of Churches and Christian Workers was formed, which in its 1905 annual convention called for a meeting at Carnegie Hall in New York. It was held in November of that year and the constitution of the Federal Council of the Churches of Christ in America was drawn up.

The Federal Council was organized at Philadelphia in 1908 with the recognition of Jesus Christ as the Divine Lord as the only doctrinal statement. The Council was more social than theological in its interest, and its "Social Creed of the Churches" emphasized its interest in amelioration of bad conditions in economic life. It will be noted that all three of these organizations were non-creedal and dominated by men of liberal theological persuasion who found the old Evangelical Alliance creedal emphasis too binding.

The creedal emphasis was, however, to be continued along national lines by evangelicals at a later date. The American Council of Christian Churches was organized in 1941. The National Association of Evangelicals drew the inspiration for its founding from the New England Fellowship of 1929. A letter by Ralph T. Davis and a tour of 31 states in 1941 by J. Elwin Wright led to meetings of evangelical leaders in Chicago in 1941 and in St. Louis in 1942 out of which the National Association of Evangelicals emerged in 1943. Both of these national conservative organizations have a creedal basis.

International intraconfessional confederation developed early among churches with a common creedal basis. The Lambeth Conference of 1867 of Anglicans of the world began the periodic discussion of matters of common interest. The World Alliance of Churches Holding the Presbyterian System (1875), the World Methodist Council (1881), the International Council of Congregationalists (1891), the Baptist World Alliance (1905) and the World Lutheran Federation (1923) all have met regularly since their founding. These groups helped to create an interest in international interconfessional organization.

Cooperation by those of more liberal persuasion in national confederations followed three roads to a world interconfessional organization. The earliest move in this direction came with the meeting of representatives of missionary societies at the Edinburgh Missionary Conference in 1910 under the chairmanship of John R. Mott. This meeting resulted in the organization of the International Missionary Council in 1921. Because of the embarrassment of explaining denominational differences to nationals on the mission field, the appeal of this movement in which John R. Mott was so influential can be readily understood. Successive meetings of missionary organizations followed. In 1961 the International Missionary Council was merged with the World Council of Churches at New Delhi.

The second area of cooperation concerned the life and work of the church and was led by Nathan Söderblom, a teacher of the history of religion and later the primate of the national church in Sweden. A meeting at Stockholm in 1925 was followed by one at Oxford in 1937. Eastern Orthodoxy was represented for the first time in the 1925 meeting. Charles H. Brent, an American Episcopal missionary bishop in the Philippines, with financial aid from J. P. Morgan, interested over 100 churches in a meeting on faith and order at Lausanne in 1927.

These movements, with much the same membership, met at Oxford and Edinburgh in 1937. Stimulated by William Adams Brown, these meetings called for a world organization of churches. A meeting at Utrecht in 1938 resulted in a constitution for the World Council of Churches. That name was suggested by Samuel M. Cavert in a committee meeting in London in July, 1938. The organization came into being with the meeting of representatives of 146 churches from 44 countries at Amsterdam in 1948. It has since held meetings in Evanston (1954) and New Delhi (1961).

Conservatives were not far behind in organizing international interconfessional confederations, but they insisted on a creedal basis for such organizations. The American Council of Christian Churches organized the International Council of Christian Churches in 1948 at Amsterdam just before the World Council met. The National Association of Evangelicals led in the formation of the World Evangelical Fellowship at Woudschoten in 1951.

It will be evident that all of these national and international organizations have been confederate aggregations of churches or groups of Christians in which the constituent parts are sovereign and do not share their sovereignty with the larger organization as would be the case in a true federation or organic union.

Organic union has been much more limited with reunion proceeding along national intraconfessional and interconfessional lines. Those denominations with similar traditions have found it easier to unite organically. Separate Scottish Presbyterian churches came together finally in 1929 in the Kirk of Scotland. Two Presbyterian churches in the United States in 1958 formed the United Presbyterian Church in the USA. Several Methodist churches reunited in the Methodist Church in 1939.

The union in Prussia of Lutheran and Reformed churches is an early illustration of interconfessional reunion. Presbyterians, Congregationalists and Methodists of Canada merged to form the United Church of Canada in 1925. By 1947 even the Episcopalians linked with Presbyterians, Methodists and Congregationalists to form the Church of South India. In each case the uniting churches merged their identity in the new church.

This review of the story of ecumenism has some suggestions for evangelicals who are interested in unity with fellow-believers. It has been apparent that the leadership in the formation of the ecumenical movement has come largely from America during the twentieth century. Such leadership has been doctrinally latitudinarian and activistic. Matters of pragmatic concern rather than theological formulations have attracted their attention.

This is a departure from previous attempts at reunion which have emphasized creeds based on the Bible and suggests that conservative forces cooperating with each other have been more in the historical tradition when they have insisted that unity be unity in truth in order to achieve the unity of the faith (Ephesians 4:13) once delivered to the saints (Jude 3). Unity for unity's sake may lead to a union of the lowest common denominator. Truth must be considered in any attempt at confederation because creed determines conduct and faith leads to action.

The dangers of overcentralization, institutionalism and the multiplication of bureaucracy also attend any attempt at unity. The church of the Middle Ages certainly illustrates this danger. That which was an organimic instrument in the hands of God to spiritual ends became an organization which was no longer a means, but an end in itself. This also led to a perversion of doctrine, as witness the rise of the doctrines of the mass and papal infallibility. This is likely to be the experience of the World Council of Churches if it ever becomes a Protestant world church.

It is also apparent that forces in the National and World Councils have much more interest in having the churches engage in social activity than in theological discussion to find a scriptural consensus for union. Doctrinal agreement does not exclude social action, but keeps such activity realistic and not utopian. It was the evangelicals, cooperating with each other and having a doctrinal unity without organization, who did so much to spread the Gospel and bring about effective social reform in England and America in the nineteenth century.

The endangering of the separation of church and state emerges when a religious organization of churches seeks as an organization to direct governmental policy at home and abroad. This might be better done as the evangelicals did in nineteenth century Britain by extra-church organizations for a specific purpose in which both Christian and non-Christian citizens might join.

Union for the sake of union and the proliferation of organization will never fulfill the desire of Christ that His followers be one (John 17:21). Any cooperation or organization of Christians along organic and confederate lines should not lead to the sacrifice of truth nor to any fellowship which does not give allegiance to the Saviour whom we know only through the Scriptures which lead us by faith to a living experience of His reality. Perhaps American evangelicals under God can lead in the creation of such scriptural unity.

Chapter Five

ECUMENISM IN THE LIGHT OF CHURCH HISTORY

Earle E. Cairns

Evangelicals who have given consideration to contemporary church history know that there are strong international organizations, such as the World Council of Churches, and national groups, such as the National Council of Churches, which tend to identify the drive for ecumenism with their particular organizations.

Distinction must be made, however, between the ecumenical spirit and the ecumenical organization. It was evangelicals, it will be remembered, who in 1846 translated the ecumenical spirit into the Evangelical Alliance, an organization with a creedal basis. Disunity was introduced by the liberal elements in the Alliance who were dissatisfied with the creedal approach and who set up other organizations culminating in the Federal Council of Churches. They made cooperative service rather than cooperative faith the basis for unity.

The translation of the ecumenical spirit into concrete reality raises the question of how this shall be accomplished. Evangelicals unite with others in Christendom in the desire to realize the kind of unity for which Christ prayed in John 17, but they are not ready to admit that the unity of that great prayer can be limited to any human organization. They want to ask questions about the message, machinery, mission and motivation essential to fulfillment of Christ's prayer for unity of His own.

I

The question of *focus* is important. We do not want an ecumenical organization which will only outwardly represent Christian unity nor an organization which in spirit has a different focus from that demanded of us by God. This involves consideration of the foundation and faith which underlie our search for spiritual unity

66

in concrete form. This seems to have been forgotten in the frenzied rush to have an organizational ecumenical expression.

Paul links love with truth in the phrase "speaking the truth in love" (Ephesians 4:15). Truth is not to be sacrificed to some sentimental consideration which we characterize as "love." Ecumenical enthusiasts of whatever persuasion must answer the question as to what authority and what beliefs should underlie organizational expression of the ecumenical spirit.

The *foundation* of true Christian unity must be determined if such unity is to be a reality in spirit as well as in machinery. The problem of authority has been a primary consideration throughout ecclesiastical history. The Roman Catholic Church makes the church, speaking through its head, the pope, the infallible authority for faith and morals. Of course, in deciding what are acceptable doctrinal and moral standards the testimony of Scripture and tradition is given great weight.

Others who reject an institutional center of authority might suggest an emotional aspect of human life as authority. The early Quakers made the "inner light" — the operation of the Holy Spirit in the individual Christian's breast — the final authority. Thus the "openings" which they received had as much validity as the writings of Paul so long as they did not contradict the secondary standards of Scripture or reason. Neo-orthodoxy, with its emphasis upon the Bible becoming the Word of God in a subjective crisis of the soul created by the Holy Spirit illumining some part of the Bible, tends to fall into this category.

Still others locate authority in human reason and would subordinate everything to the test of rationality. The liberal movement which decided that the Bible "contained" the Word of God used reason to determine just what parts should be authoritative in the light of the rational presuppositions of Biblical criticism. The movement, which reached its greatest peak in nineteenth century Germany, helped to spawn a Hitler who offered the German people a new center of authority — the Volk — which was supposed to express its spirit through Der Fuehrer who was the soul of the Volk.

The objective historical revelation of the Bible rather than institutional, emotional or rational authorities must be for evangelicals the foundation and judge of any ecumenical conversation.

We have already seen in the history of the church that until the twentieth century in America all endeavors to create unity in Christendom were based upon the foundation of the authority of the Bible. This is why the early church fathers made so much of apostolic succession. The best guarantee that they were following the mandates of the living Word, Christ, before the written Word was completed and canonized was to have leaders who were in the line of succession from the apostles who received the oral Gospel at the mouth of Christ and who later under the inspiration of the Holy Spirit put it into written form. Leaders with the authoritative message would protect them from heretics and schism. Paul in Acts 17:2 and I Corinthians 15:3-4 uses the expression, "according to the Scriptures," meaning the Old Testament. This foundation would guarantee the veracity of his message about Christ's death and resurrection.

None of the ecumenical organizations except those of evangelicals have paid much attention to the Scriptures as a foundation for unity. The Federal Council and its successor, the National Council, ignore the Scriptures in any official statement. Not until the New Delhi meeting in 1961 did the World Council get around to adding the phrase, "according to the Scriptures," to its brief theological statement. Various statements by the leaders and in the literature of the WCC give justifiable concern as to whether by this they mean an objective revelation from God by the Holy Spirit through men or a subjective record by good men which becomes the Word of God or contains the Word of God. Too little attention has been given to what is meant by the phrase "according to the Scriptures" and too much to latitudinarian expressions which leave the matters of what Scripture is and how it is to be used to the discretion of the churches and individuals in the organization.

Ecumenists should recognize that the church has always given attention to authority in ecumenical conversation until the twentieth century when it was minimized. Paul, who categorically states that Scripture was inspired of God, relates it as foundation to salvation, sanctification and service (II Timothy 3:15-17). Christ is "the truth" as well as the way and the life (John 14:6). The central ecumenical issue in the Reformation, that of authority, is still an important issue. What is truth is still dependent upon where is truth. Even the favorite verse of the ecumenists — John 17:21 — rests upon truth. That word is used in verses 17 and 19. It is a perversion of words to twist the chapter into support of physical organization. Its intent is a spiritual organism similar to the relation between the Father and the Son based upon truth which the Spirit will give the apostles (John 16:13; 14:17, 26) in order that others may believe (John 17:21).

The evangelical will not disdain dialogue, but he should insist in a spirit of love that the question of authority which is transhuman is fundamental in any consideration of ecumenism. Beliefs always have some *locus* of authority from which they are drawn, be they institutional, emotional or rational. The American Council of Christian Churches and the National Association of Evangelicals have both wisely insisted upon the fully inspired Scriptures as the basic foundation for association and creed. We know nothing historically of Christ apart from the Scriptures except for a few scattered extrabiblical historical references.

Upon the foundation of the Scriptures, *faith* in the sense of creed can be constructed. Biblical doctrine has by human reflection been systematized into rules of faith, such as those of Irenaeus and Tertullian, and systematic theology. This in turn has become the basis for dogma which is the consensus of what men believe the Scriptures teach. Conduct always springs from an implicit or explicit creed, action from faith, work from belief. In each case these will be found to rest upon a book, the Bible. Islam's conduct is derived from the Koran; the Nazi theorists looked to Hegel, Darwin and Nietzsche for their beliefs, and the Marxists are fanatical followers of Karl Marx whose *Communist Manifesto* and *Das Kapital* constitute their Bible. In the absence of a strong theological creed, even the Federal Council drew up a "Social Creed." The question is not union in service, but a union which reflects "the unity of the faith" (Ephesians 4:13).

Paul states in Acts 17:2-3 and I Corinthians 15:3-4 the irreducible elements in any creedal statement, viz., the death and resurrection of Christ for our sins. This cannot involve less than His incarnation and virgin birth which constitute Him as God. Such was the judgment of the great ecumenical councils, such as Nicaea in 325 and Chalcedon in 451. It also involves His substitutionary atonement for the church which He has "purchased with his own blood" (Acts 20:28). Churchmen until the twentieth century — with its creedal and doctrinal latitudinarianism — have always insisted that creed was important. Even such humanists as Grotius, who advocated a union of Christendom, insisted upon the Scriptures as authority and upon a minimal creed concerning Christ's deity and atonement. Evangelicals who want a basic creed for unity are more in the historical tradition than those who minimize authority and creed in ecumenical conversation.

Basic beliefs have had short shrift in ecumenical organizations other than those led and supported by evangelicals. The phrase, "Divine Lord and Saviour," constituted the only creedal statement beyond the Social Creed of the Federal Council of Churches. The preamble to the constitution drawn up in 1905 states that in God's Providence the hour has come when it seems fitting to manifest unity in "Jesus Christ as Divine Lord and Saviour, by the creation of an inclusive cooperative agency of the Christian churches of the United States of America." Organization is to be the way then in which ecumenical unity is to express itself.

The minimal creedal statement of the World Council is an improvement over these statements of the national American ecumenical organization. Until the New Delhi meeting in 1961 the churches of the WCC stated that they "accept our Lord Jesus Christ as God and Saviour." The patronizing word, "accept," was replaced by "confess" in 1961. Unfortunately the "Explanatory Memorandum" of the Provisional Committee of the World Council of Churches stated that the Council was not concerned "with the manner in which the churches interpret them." One may be trinitarian, but does he do justice to the early ecumenical formulations of the doctrine of the God-Man?

Theodore Wedel, who strongly supports the World Council and seems to want it to become a federal organization, is still of the opinion that Christian unity cannot "be other than a unity of faith," without which the idea of church is "ultimately meaningless." He finds this revelation of faith in "the acts of God" and this "revelation of God in history" is "enshrined in the Bible."[1] Surely if the WCC is serious in its desire, it should be able to accept sincerely the historic formulations of the Apostles' Creed and the Nicene Creed as minimal statements of faith. Roman Catholic and Orthodox churches and evangelical Protestant churches have no trouble with these formulations.

Charles Foster in his scholarly *An Errand of Mercy* has demonstrated that before the Civil War in America — and also in England — evangelicals of different faiths worked together amicably to destroy slavery and other social ills because they united on a "central essential core of Christian faith."[2] Effective unity can be nothing less than a unity of faith. Acceptance of the lowest common denominator will never build a lasting ecumenical organization or spirit that adequately fulfills John 17:21.

II

The *form* in which the ecumenical spirit can legitimately express itself naturally follows consideration of its focus in an adequate foundation and faith. How are freedom and unity to be reconciled in the essential machinery? Several alternatives for ecumenical cooperation suggest themselves and have been used at various times in the history of the modern church.

Fellowship in informal meetings is one possibility. Any Christian who has participated in the Billy Graham campaigns or other ventures without formal organizational structure of the churches can testify to the ecumenical fellowship that he sensed in such meetings. Prayer groups across denominational lines have been fruitful. This, however, is too ephemeral to suit those bent on ecumenical organization, and it is not adequately organized for continuing cooperation.

During the nineteenth century, *interdenominational cooperation* thrived and cooperative associations were developed in large numbers. Many are still functioning; among them, the American Bible Society. Protestants and other Americans United for Separation of Church and State (POAU) is a recent organization of this type which has enlisted the efforts of Christians across denominational lines to protect our historic and wise separation of church and state.

But many prefer closer integration than this and favor a *confederate* type of ecumenical organization. A confederation brings together representatives of constituent bodies to discuss and act upon matters of common interest, but in each case the member body retains its sovereignty and the acts of the group are not binding upon it unless it so decides. This was the form of government of our country under the Articles of Confederation from 1781 until 1789.

This is also the form which ecumenical organization has taken. The National Council of Churches and the National Association of Evangelicals are technically confederations. The old Federal Council was technically misnamed. The WCC and the World Evangelical Fellowship are correctly described as confederations of churches. Each group is sovereign but cooperates in matters of common interest. Archbishop Temple's "Explanatory Memorandum" stated that it was not a federation and its Assembly and Central Committee had "no constitutional authority whatsoever" over the churches in it. It is "only consultative and cannot legislate" for the churches. It has duties without rights. This is as true of evangelical ecumenical organizations as it is of the World Council.

Confederate organization seems to be a wise approach because it does not destroy the rights of the sovereign constituent denominations, churches or individual members. Thus there need be no compromising lowest common denominator of authority or creed. It also serves to protect the historic doctrine of separation of church and state without preventing Christians from acting together on humanitarian, social, political and economic matters. The First Amendment to the Constitution of the United States does not bar cooperative Christian citizenship expressed through cooperative groups which are seeking to express the grass roots will of their constituency. It only bars an established, privileged or favored church. NAE will be wise not to go beyond the confederate type of organization in which so far the spirit of real ecumenism based on an agreed foundation and faith has expressed itself.

Many non-evangelicals, however, desire *organic unity* in which the constituent parts either share their sovereignty with the central organization in the merger or give up all sovereignty to the central organization and disappear as separate entities. This could take two forms — corporate federal or unitary church union.

The first of these would be similar to the government of the United States in which the states and federal government have spheres of sovereignty granted by the Constitution with which the other cannot interfere. States cannot coin money, set tariffs or conduct foreign relations, but they are sovereign in such things as education.

Some ecumenical thinkers seem to desire an organic federal unity in "a strong federation combined with full intercommunion." This would bring limitation upon the sovereignty of churches in the World Council and would give to the Assembly rights as well as duties.

A *corporate unitary organization,* however, would involve machinery in which the constituent parts would disappear. This would eliminate denominations. Britain is a unitary monarchy. There are no states and the counties are administrative units. This would mean, if put into effect, that the World Council of Churches would become the World Church. Denominations would cease to exist as separate entities and merge in a monolithic organization. Such an organization would become an institution seeking to perpetuate itself. It would also be in danger of increasing dictatorial centralization and bureaucracy. In order to prevent revolution it would have to become so inclusivistic that it would give up creed and authority in Scripture.

Thus far the dream of a world church is only a dream. But the dedication of its devotees makes it a frightening possibility.

Evangelicals will do well to remember these things and to favor confederate ecumenical organization rather than organic federal or unitary ecumenism. Unity must always be based upon present doctrinal and spiritual accord. The phrase, "of one accord," used so often in Acts by Luke suggests this kind of spiritual unity which should never be lost in organizational union.

III

The fuzziness of many who want ecumenical unity becomes apparent when the question is raised concerning the *function* of such organization. What is the mission which ecumenism is to fulfill? Union in service is hardly enough to make that the main function of an ecumenical spirit because it may lead to the lowest common denominator in theology.

Witnessing or the proclamation of the Gospel for conversion of the non-Christian should be the first aim of the ecumenical spirit in view of Christ's own commission to the church. While He promises to be with the church all through the age (Matthew 28:18-20), it is in connection with its primary task of evangelism. The Scriptures make it clear that the proclamation of Christ's death and resurrection as the sovereign remedy for individual sin is the main task of the church.[3] One must be a *marturia* (witness) of the *kerygma*.

It is at this point that neo-evangelicals must be careful in their desire to make Christianity relevant to culture. This must not take precedence over Christ's commission to preach the Gospel.

Likewise many of the ardent ecumenists should rethink their emphasis upon unity in service which raises the question as to how well they are fulfilling Christ's commission. Dr. Harold Lindsell of Fuller Theological Seminary has ably demonstrated through a study that, even though the ecumenical spirit first manifested itself on the mission field, foreign missionary enterprises on the part of those denominations that have formed organic unions or entered into the National Council have steadily dropped until not more than a third of foreign missionaries from North America would be enrolled under this banner. At the same time the number of missionaries in evangelically oriented groups forms from one-half to two-thirds of missionary personnel going from the North American continent.[4]

Evangelicals should consider with reserve any call for ecumenical cooperation that would blunt the imperative of world evangelization as Christ's first and final command to the church. The Christian is primarily an ambassador for Christ (II Corinthians 5:20) in a world of syncretistic religion, messianic totalitarianism, and humanistic relativism.

Having said this, we should not forget that the Scriptures suggest the second function of the ecumenical spirit should be *loving service* on the part of the Christian to his fellows and to the unregenerated. Such is the order which Paul suggests in Galatians 6:10, Ephesians 2:10 and Titus 3:8. Faith which leads one to witness is also to be manifested in *diakonia*. Remember that the disciples of Antioch sent economic relief by the hands of Paul and Barnabas to the famine-stricken church in Jerusalem. Christians through the ages have been generous in relieving the needs of the poor. They have also fought entrenched evils.

Faith in Christ demands that we demonstrate Christian love in making the Gospel relevant to the needs of those around us. The over-emphasis of the social gospel on service and our own strong emphasis on eschatology which causes us to believe that we are near the end of the age should not blind us to these demands of the Gospel upon us. Faith expressed in loving service will open many doors closed to the Gospel.

Fellowship or *koinonia,* which has been greatly emphasized by the ecumenists, is the third function of the ecumenical spirit. Evangelicals would agree with this, but naturally raise the question as to the nature of this fellowship. Fellowship in the New Testament is always rooted in a spiritual relationship to Christ which puts one into proper relationship with fellow believers. This is the emphasis in I John 1:3, 6-7; 5:1.

The history of the church indicates that many times separation is essential. Adherence to truth should not be sacrificed for the sake of a sentimental Christian fellowship which has no real spiritual foundation. Christ in Matthew 18:15-17, Paul in I Corinthians 5:4-5, and John in II John 7-11 command separation from evil brethren with a view to awaking them to repentance. Desire for fellowship should not blind us to the demand for allegiance to Biblical truth on the part of those who ask us to fellowship with them.

The present ecumenical spirit of togetherness seems to blur the edges of truth. Fellowship is basically a matter of the spirit, and no twentieth century hail-fellow well-met spirit is an adequate substitute for it. On the other hand, evangelicals should be ready for fellowship with any who are truly Christ's and adhere to His Word even though in some points we may disagree with them.

Love or *agape* to the brethren should be the fourth factor in any ecumenical cooperation. While we hold to the truth, we should do it in love (Ephesians 4:15). It is at this point that many fundamentalists fail. Loving toleration of those with different, even false, views does not mean compromise. Toleration should not be confused with compromise. An irenic spirit can be coupled with a spirited defense of the faith. Gibbon, the eighteenth century rationalist historian who studied the reason for the decline and fall of the

Roman Empire, pays tribute to the manifestation of love by Christians as an important factor in their conquest of that empire.

I have deliberately left *unity* as the last function of the ecumenical movement because any unity that is not based on fulfillment of the foregoing functions is not real unity. Christ is the only real foundation (I Corinthians 3:11) for unity, and any unity which does not recognize His headship in the spiritual organism which is the church can never create real or lasting cooperation. Unity among Christians will help unbelievers come to Christ only if that unity is based upon fellowship among regenerated and Bible-believing Christians who lovingly serve their fellows.

IV

If such are the functions of a true ecumenism, what should be the *force* or motivation of such unity? Dr. Visser't Hooft quotes Zinzendorf's opinion that fellowship which is only based on "agreement of opinions and forms without a change of heart" is dangerous.[5] Evangelicals would agree with this wholeheartedly because a spirit of revival which changes lives has always had ecumenical results. Organization can never be a substitute for revival.

Even in so strong a period of doctrinal controversy as the Reformation, evangelicals did cooperate in many ways, and if there were not too vital differences they came together as in the case of the followers of Zwingli and Calvin. Evangelicals in the Church of England and Nonconformists cooperated wholeheartedly in social reform from 1790 to 1837. Devereux Jarratt and Francis Asbury cooperated in revival efforts in the South about 1775. The great number of extra-church organizations which sprang up after the Civil War to unite Christians in service were results of revival. It was in the revivalistic atmosphere of Moody's Northfield that the Student Volunteer Movement was formed. Real ecumenism can only come out of revival which is the sovereign work of the Holy Spirit.

Any real union should be one of regenerated Christians. They can even cooperate with others who are not Christians in extra-church organizations for common desired ends which are in accord with Biblical truth and Christian love. They can do this without sacrificing doctrinal purity or Christian love. But the invisible church will never become one in reality unless it is limited to the visible church, a rather utopian prospect.

Perhaps the ecumenists would get farther if they adopted Acts 2:42 and Ephesians 4:3-6 as their blueprint for union. Certainly evangelicals should hold to this as an absolute minimum in ecumenical dialogue. Only then will "the unity of the Spirit in the bond of peace" become a reality.

Chapter Six

EVANGELICALS, ECUMENICAL COUNCILS and ETERNITY

Clyde W. Taylor

Sometime ago 32 Siberian evangelical Christians turned up at the American embassy in Moscow seeking help as they struggled to live their faith under the oppression of Communism. The tragic event — for the inability of our diplomats to help them made it that — made headlines in this country and that word "evangelical" stood out as big as life.

Though we have had no direct contact with the refugees before or since that time, one thing became abundantly clear to us. These were our brothers and sisters in Christ. They identified themselves as "evangelical" Christians and NAE actions in the case were largely determined by that fact. Through a cable NAE interceded directly with the Kremlin on their behalf and offered to assume total responsibility for getting the entire group to the United States and rehabilitating them if the Russian government would let them go.

Needless to say, we received no reply. We could hardly have expected one. But this one dramatic incident serves to illustrate the plight of hundreds of thousands of Christians who live in a modern form of captivity much like that of Moses' time or the later Babylonian period. Our God is a great Deliverer, however, and sooner or later the time will come when He will deliver His people from bondage.

In the meantime we remember that we are united with those who serve Jesus Christ behind the Iron and Bamboo Curtains. We sense this unity even though we cannot trace it through any organizational ties. Indeed, true Christian unity does not depend on formal organizational relationships. This does not mean that it is only a theoretical thing, for it frequently calls for implementation and this requires organizations of one kind or another. The organizations, however, are the effect and not the cause. Our evangelical fellowship — just witness that which bridges geographic barriers and man-made curtains — is not dependent upon them.

I

In order to communicate the truth of this to those with little evangelical background, it is frequently necessary for us to spend a little time orienting them. They need to know who evangelicals are and to understand what makes them that way. We must help them be acquainted with our theology, understand our witness, and appreciate our mission.

When I am asked to define "evangelical" I say simply that an evangelical is one who believes in and, we trust, witnesses to the "evangel," or the Gospel of Jesus Christ. This Gospel can be spelled out clearly as that which Jesus Christ has done for us by His death and resurrection, giving us eternal life by grace through faith.

Evangelical theology always starts out by affirming that our final and complete authority is the Bible, the Word of God. Then we go on to other things. We believe in the Trinity. We believe in the deity of Jesus Christ, in His sinless life, in His atoning death, in His bodily resurrection, in His second coming. We believe that we are born again — regenerated — by the work of the Holy Spirit in our lives and that we are equipped for service as He fills us. We believe in the unity of the saints in one spiritual body.

This is the simple, uncluttered evangelical theology. This much binds us together. If you believe that much with all your heart, we will see each other in heaven. And if we are going to be together in heaven, we might as well establish some relationship now and get used to the idea!

Our basic beliefs are important to us. We cannot give them up, not for any amount of union or united effort, if this be required of us. Rev. Jack Dain, missionary secretary of the Anglican Church in Australia, told evangelical leaders in India recently that above all else evangelicals must maintain their theological integrity.[1]

I do not see how you can define an evangelical without referring to the entire New Testament as the authority or to some statement of faith that pinpoints the matter of personal belief. I will readily grant that there is a great diversity among evangelicals on some points, but at the center there are these historic Christian doctrines on which there is complete concurrence.

That then is our evangelical theology. What is our witness? Is it social? (We are certainly in an overseas relief program in a big way.) Is it educational? (Schools started by missionary organizations abound.) Is it medical? (Hospitals staffed by Christian personnel can be found everywhere.) These are all important ministries, but they are not the heart of our evangelical witness. Its basic thrust is spiritual, aimed at changing the nature of man.

Let me use India for an example. When I went there a number of years ago to stimulate interest in cooperative evangelical action I had been assured that it was an impossible situation. I faced about 150 church leaders and sensed the suspicion with which they greeted my mission.

What do you think is our main need in India? they asked me. If I had said organizational unity, some would have agreed with me. A call for more training would have struck a responsive chord with others. A plea for cooperative social action would probably have gotten one or two affirmative nods.

But I answered, "Revival in the church." And I saw them all relax. They were for this. They knew India needed revival. "But how do you think we are going to achieve it?" they asked. I told them there was only one way — the Bible way, by prayer and seeking God's face. Thus the Evangelical Fellowship of India was started with a spiritual emphasis which it has maintained through the years. They still pray every day at noon across that subcontinent. Only God knows how many hundreds of thousands pause at that moment to pray in many languages and dialects for revival in India. And this is one of the things that has made EFI a strong, dynamic force.

While our primary emphasis must be spiritual, we must seek for ways of expression. Evangelism is perhaps the first of these. In India evangelicals have found that you can't pray for revival without doing something about it. Cooperative and lay evangelism go forward there as in Latin America. And there is the theological school at Yeotmal, India, in which — believe it or not — seventeen denominations cooperate without the compromise of doctrines or distinctives. This is legitimate, true evangelical ecumenism. Not compromise. Not union. Just unity.

But the thing that gives impetus and direction to our witness is our evangelical mission. What are we trying to do? What is our goal? I think the Bible spells it out rather clearly — preach the Gospel to every creature! We are to take the good news to every nation, tongue and tribe. As I watch the reports of the progress of the translation of the Bible into other languages, it is interesting to note that almost all of the linguistic work is being done by evangelicals. Our mission gives us a concern for those without God's Word.

Our mission is to be used of the Holy Spirit as God finishes the task of calling out a people for His name. James reminds the apostolic council in Acts 15:14 that God had started a process through which He was calling out from the Gentiles a people for His name. This process is still going on, and our mission and purpose is to be a part of it.

II

And what shall we say about ecumenical councils? After all the space that was given in the world press to the Second Vatican Council, we should probably consider it first. We haven't seen any direct results produced by the Council yet. All we have is trends — and one tremendous struggle.

It is rather common knowledge that the Vatican Council has developed into two camps — liberal against conservative. The tangible results of this historic gathering, which could last several years, will depend on which group wins control of the machinery. If the liberals come out on top, some significant changes can be expected. The dogmas of the church will not be altered, of course, but it is possible that the mass might be put into local languages and some changes might be made in the celibacy rules as regards the priesthood.

But if the conservative *Curia*, dominated by Italians, continues in control with the backing of some of the hierachy in this country, they will maintain that the Roman Catholic Church is a changeless church and things will continue the same. The death of Pope John

XXIII and the election of a new pope will have a profound effect on the conservative-liberal struggle.

The wishful thinking of some naive Protestants nothwithstanding, the Second Vatican Council is not likely to produce results that will make a Protestant-Catholic union an early possibility. Some Protestants seem to drool at the prospect of becoming one with Rome again, but having been a missionary in Latin America I can assure you there is no enthusiasm for this south of the border.

However, this Council has created one amazing by-product. The ecumenical winds have blown some unbelievable freedoms to Spain. All but three or four of the long-closed Protestant churches are now open. Evangelical marriages are being allowed. Some soldiers imprisoned for not kneeling at the mass have been freed. Evangelicals have been promised liberty to have their own publishing houses and schools. There is no doubt that the changing climate in Spain is a reflection of the Vatican Council on the Spanish hierarchy.

Now what about the World Council of Churches, the Protestant "ecumenical council." It is difficult to speak definitively about that organization because there are so few official statements that can be drawn upon for interpretation. There are books galore, but not many which contain official policy.

At the end of the 1961 session, the Council listed 198 member denominations and claimed 300 million members. Of these, some 94 million belong to non-reformed, Orthodox churches. Thus the WCC as a religious entity is a mixed multitude. Without doubt it has millions of evangelicals in its membership. They are not there by personal choice, but because their denominations belong and they do not feel constrained to leave their churches. These faithful believers would be at one end of the WCC spectrum.

In the middle you will find a countless number of church members who couldn't care less about anything religious as long as it doesn't make too many demands on their lives. They have unquestioningly followed their leaders into the world organization.

At the other end of the spectrum are those in the non-reformed, sacramental churches who have never been told that as individuals they must make a direct and personal approach to God through Jesus Christ in order to find salvation. No one knows how many —

or how few — of them have been born again. And it is at this point
that evangelicals become immediately concerned. How can you
have spiritual fellowship with people who are spiritually dead?

But perhaps the goal of the World Council of Churches is of
more significance to evangelicals than its makeup. The Council
characterizes itself as being nothing more than an international fellowship of national church bodies. And it is almost impossible to
conclusively prove otherwise. All you can do is quote some of the
leaders, but some of these statements give substance to what critics
of the Council have been saying since it was first formed. For example, a dispatch from the 1961 New Delhi meeting quoted
Rev. Kenneth Slack, who is executive secretary of the British Council
of Churches, as referring to "the coming great church."[2] When this
phrase was first used by an evangelical leader in the early days of
the movement, it was heatedly refuted by the ecumenical leadership.
Now it crops up occasionally in the ecumenical vocabulary.

While in Africa early in 1962 I picked up a report of an address
given by Bishop Zulu, an Anglican bishop in one of the provinces
and a member of the executive committee of the World Council of
Churches. He said among other things that the unity which they
are seeking is "a unity which makes of the churches a Church."

Union seems to be one of the main goals of the Council which
officially claims for itself to be nothing more than "a fellowship that
confesses the Lord Jesus Christ as God and Saviour according to the
Scriptures and therefore seeks to fulfill together their common calling to the glory of the one God, Father, Son and Holy Spirit." And
it seems that everywhere union is effected under the ecumenical
banner it takes on the form of an episcopacy with apostolic succession of the clergy and the Anglican ritual of administering the
sacraments. So much is this true that an Anglican leader in India
said not long ago that it was a most disappointing thing to see the
churches unite, take on the form of the Anglican Church, put on
the robes of the Anglicans, but have no spiritual life inside the shell.[3]

If union of the churches is the unofficial goal of the WCC,
what is its theology? Its only creed is that one stated above, and
with each member free to interpret it in his own way, the only real
function the statement seems to serve is to exclude the Unitarians
who find themselves unable to go along with its trinitarian com-

mitment. The Council will take arch-conservatives and arch-liberals and you can put your own interpretation on the "statement of faith."

But it has no theology — that is, no definable theology. It could be syncretism for the Asian wing seems to want to take the best of all the world's religions and compile a sort of ethical code. Or it could be universalism for this seems to be the direction of the European wing. It has been estimated by a responsible authority that more than 90 per cent of the European clergy are universalists in some degree. If I believed that everyone is going to heaven anyhow but that I still ought to work for God somehow, I would probably do exactly what the ecumenists have done — go into the organizing business. All that would be left to do is establish a manifestation of Christian "oneness" and get the people outside committed to join the organization. To do this you don't need a theology.

The message and program of the WCC is dual. The first part urges the churches to repent of their divisions and form national unions. The ideal, to their way of thinking, is to have one Church of Christ in every country. This is the present thrust in the Congo and so sure are they of success that the stationery is already printed and the name is in prominent use throughout the country even though the church doesn't yet exist.

There are two serious dangers inherent in this kind of monopolistic practice. One is the threat to missionary activity. A top evangelical leader in one South Asian country who was totally submerged in ecumenical ideals and thinking refused entrance to a mission board because the missionaries would not promise to make every convert a member of the national church. The interesting aspect of this particular situation is that no national church existed at that time, but this leader would not allow a new work to be established unless it followed the ecumenical pattern. Another danger of having just one church in a country is that it could be controlled by giving or withholding financial support. Such an approach was made to national church leaders in Vietnam by the World Council of Churches. Their respresentatives went to Saigon, bypassed the missionaries of the Christian and Missionary Alliance — the only church of any size in that country — and made the national leaders a direct offer to provide assistance in a hospital, rebuilding churches, pastors' salaries and scholarships for their students in return for cooperation with the WCC. This method of securing cooperation is certainly open to question and even the motives in this case are suspect.

The second part of the message of the Council urges the churches to have a witness in society — that is, participate in the political and social life and in the revolutionary reforms of the nation. This is their way of implementing the social gospel. An observer at the All-Africa Christian Youth Assembly held early in 1963 under ecumenical auspices reported that "the three themes of unity, Africanization and political involvement were emphasized to the exclusion of almost any other consideration in the plenary sessions."

He said he feared that "if the delegates act as encouraged to do in their local situation, they will incite much 'revolutionary' behavior among youth and create serious and disruptive tensions in local churches."[4]

Except in the obvious case of Vietnam mentioned earlier, I do not want to impugn the motives of the ecumenical leaders. They are sincere, determined men. It is a stark tragedy that their tremendous drive and energy are directed in such shallow channels that do not flow into some eternal reservoir.

III

Eternity, you see, is going to be the final measuring stick of everything we do — all the great superstructures we build, whether evangelical or ecumenical, will end one day at the trumpet sound. Many of the things on which we spend so much time, money and effort now will not mean one thing then. This may surprise some people, but the National Association of Evangelicals is not going to heaven — not as an organization. None of these other great world bodies are going to be there either — not as a structured entity.

But Christ's body is going to be there, gathered out of every kindred, tongue, tribe and nation.

As I have read book after book in which the authors rapturously talk about building the church, I have been amazed that none of them mention that it is going to heaven. But that is its ultimate destiny, this invisible Church Universal embracing all believers. Paul assures us of this in II Corinthians 4:17-18: "For our light affliction, which is but for a moment, worketh for us a far more exceeding and eternal weight of glory; while we look not at the things which are seen, but at the things which are not seen: for the things which are seen are temporal; but the things which are not seen are eternal."

And then I think about God's Word which so many today question and subjugate to human reason until they have no authority at all. It is going to be in heaven. When all is said and done man's foolishness will be gone, but God's Word is eternal. Jesus Himself is our authority for this: "Heaven and earth shall pass away; but my words shall shall not pass away" (Mark 13:31).

And of course every believer in Jesus Christ is going to be in heaven. Jesus promised this in John 5:24: "Verily, verily, I say unto you, He that heareth my word, and believeth on him that sent me, hath everlasting life, and shall not come into condemnation; but is passed from death unto life." I think about a little widow in the Congo whom I heard about. She had won 800 people in one village to Christ. She will be up there in this Church Eternal, and she will have 800 units with her. All one with us now in Christ, race and color notwithstanding. This is unity.

Rev. Leith Samuel, a pastor in London, England, wrote recently:

> The Church of Jesus Christ is going to be completed, gathered out of every tribe and tongue and people and nation as believers built in the power of the Holy Spirit upon the rock of Christ in the Holy Scriptures. The sand of human tradition and theological compromise offers no firm foundation upon which to build. There are many signs that the storm of divine judgment is gathering to break upon our Christ-rejecting civilization. We cannot afford to spend too long in discussing ways and means of achieving unity while men and women under sentence of death are waiting for the word of deliverance and the good news of the free grace of God. If a passion for Christ and for souls came from the Holy Ghost upon our feeble generation of believers, our ecclesiastical uncertainties would be resolved like mists before the rising sun. Wilt thou not revive us again, O Lord, that thy people may rejoice in Thee?[5]

Chapter Seven

IMPLEMENTING OUR EVANGELICAL UNITY

Clyde W. Taylor

The very fact that there is a strong tendency in many sections of the Protestant world to substitute the ways and means of achieving Christian unity for the preaching of the Gospel itself demands that evangelicals determine what they should do to implement their unity. The high priestly prayer of our Lord Jesus Christ in John 17:21 is not there to be ignored. At the same time, the previous chapters in this book have highlighted the fact that this verse is not talking about organizational union. We also concur that in this prayer our Lord was far more concerned about our spiritual relationship with Him and with the Father and then among ourselves than He was in any visible manifestation of it.

Having said all this, we would still have to admit that the Lord expects us to do something to make this spiritual oneness visible. So let us examine (1) what has been done to implement Christian unity, (2) what some of the problems are which impede the implementation, and (3) what is and should be our strategy for achieving this practical expression.

I

For most Protestants the beginning of any effort at worldwide cooperation and fellowship would be dated back to the formation of the International Missionary Council in the 1920's. There is a possibility it would go back to the great missionary conference at Edinburgh in 1910. However, we are aware that long before these there were movements which demonstrated the possibility of evangelical ecumenism. The Evangelical Alliance was established in England in 1846. Little by little this spread over onto the continent and even across the Atlantic to North America. Eventually the World Evangelical Alliance composed of national alliances in a

87

large number of countries was established. These alliances all had a statement of faith and were theological in content. They were composed mostly of individuals and were not organized on a council basis.

Moving into this century, the International Missionary Council was without a doubt the product or eventual result of the great conference at Edinburgh. It should be noted that the IMC was a non-theological body. It did not have a statement of faith as a basis of cooperation. Its members were national councils composed, in almost every case, of missions in the missionary lands and of church denominations in the Protestant lands.

The fact that it was not a theological body offered no major problem at the start because liberalism was just becoming a threatening factor, and was largely limited to the churches of Europe and America. It had not yet had its impact on the overseas churches. However, this movement was not long free from problems. In a number of cases the national Christian councils that were established started cooperative efforts such as Sunday school literature and the publishing of books. Immediately highlighted were the great variations and lack of unity at the theological level.

Some national councils, of course, preceded the IMC. The earliest of these was the Congo Protestant Council, established by the leaders of the Protestant missions in the Congo for purposes of representation to the Belgian government. Then one after another, but mainly in Asia, Europe and the United States, other councils or foreign mission agencies were established. Originally in the United States it was the Foreign Missions Conference. All of these cooperated with the International Missionary Council.

However, as theology and liberalism entered the picture it was soon noted that new councils or alliances, especially those formed in Africa and Latin America, did not affiliate with the International Missionary Council. Part of the reason was that evangelical missions and their churches would not cooperate if they did affiliate and in order to get a wide representation at the national level the agencies which were pro-IMC deferred in favor of evangelicals. The result is that a majority of the councils in Africa and Latin America were not related to the International Missionary Council and so are not related to its parallel body in the World Council of Churches.

Following the establishment of the IMC, other world organizations were begun, such as the World Council on Christian Education and the World Sunday School Association. This tied together the national organizations of Christian education and has continued to function as a parallel body of the World Council of Churches. Legally it is a separate organization. Actually, due to its overlapping leadership and directors, it functions as the religious education arm of the ecumenical movement.

Also organized was the World Christian Student Federation. This agency had its origin about the same time and place as the Inter-Varsity Christian Fellowship, but became the student arm of the more liberal segment of Protestantism. Actually the World Christian Student Federation operating in most Christian lands and in practically all mission fields has done much to train the leadership for what is now known as the "ecumenical movement." Such men as Dr. W. A. Visser't Hooft received their early training in the student federation.

All of these early movements had within them large segments of true evangelicals who remained true to the faith in their doctrine and message. The movements, however, were caught up in the enthusiasm to seek an organizational answer to the unity prayer of Christ. The present World Council of Churches is the tangible result.

Doubtless the motivations in the hearts and minds of its founders were many and varied. It is easy to believe that some of them had only spiritual motives and objectives in view and believed that this world organization would facilitate a more rapid evangelization of the world. It appears that still others were more concerned with the organizational benefits which would accrue and the fact that a united front would impress the world. Finally, there were certainly some who saw possibilities of great ecclesiastical power and pursued it avidly. Now, because of the fact that the International Missionary Council has been absorbed into the World Council of Churches, we have seen this cycle to a large degree completed. There are, however, subsequent problems that we shall consider.

Recently within evangelical circles there have been other movements. In 1943 Chicago witnessed the organization of the National Association of Evangelicals. Starting as a prayer meeting about two years previously and planned at a conference in St. Louis in 1942,

NAE became a constitutional entity in April 1943. The purpose back of NAE was to bring together in fellowship and cooperation for united witness and voice, as well as for necessary action, a large number of the smaller denominations in the United States. By actual count there were at least 65 different groups represented at the Chicago meeting in 1943. Not all joined, of course, and currently 40 denominations are members of NAE while others have some of their conferences in membership.

While this was taking place in America, there was a revitalization of the Evangelical Alliance going on in Great Britain. The organization had never ceased to function, but it had lost much of its original vitality. A reorganization took place in the 1940's in which not only was board personnel and leadership changed, but attention was given to the rather loosely organized World Evangelical Alliance. The British organization announced that it would no longer serve as headquarters for the world movement.

In the meantime there were numerous evangelical alliances still left on the continent, usually small in membership, dominated by a few outstanding leaders whose main program was the Universal Week of Prayer observed the first week of January each year. The alliances have continued in some countries.

Early in 1950 efforts were made from England and the United States to stimulate the formation of other alliances, fellowships or evangelical associations in parts of Europe and on the mission fields. As an outcome of this, the Evangelical Fellowship of India was organized in January 1951. Some other fellowships were proposed and in some cases partially organized in other countries of Asia. Visits were made to the evangelical alliances on the continent and there was much discussion about pulling all of these fellowships and alliances together into a world organization. The outcome of this was the founding of the World Evangelical Fellowship in Holland in August 1951. Present were representatives from approximately 21 different countries where either there were organized fellowships or alliances or where they were in the process of being formed.

A brief analysis should be made of the differences between the way evangelicals are trying to implement their unity and the concept of the World Council of Churches. As indicated in the name, the WCC is a council of church bodies. It is not like the International Missionary Council because this was an international council of councils. The WCC is composed of national church organizations. Thus Methodists in each country, Baptists, Presbyterians, etc., would join country by country with the whole denomination becoming part of the World Council. This would not necessarily mean that Baptists, Methodists or such groups in *every* country would join. It would be at the will of the national body. However, no provision was made for such groups as Congregational and Baptist churches whose polity tended to prevent their joining as a denomination. Neither was allowance made for individual churches or assemblies to join and certainly no provision for individuals to hold membership.

The original Evangelical Alliance concept was that a provision must be made for anyone who was related to Christ by the new birth to have fellowship in the movement. The outcome of this in England has been that membership in the alliance is by individuals only. In the United States when the NAE was organized this same concern was kept foremost. In other words, this fellowship of evangelicals must not do violence to the body of Christ. Born again people who would subscribe to an evangelical statement of faith should have the opportunity to fellowship. This meant that provision was made for membership at the denominational, church, regional or individual level and from the very beginning they were all welcome.

Now, with the blessing of the World Evangelical Fellowship, national fellowships around the world are being encouraged. In each case they are asked to keep in mind this principle of providing a means of fellowship to all true evangelicals. Each fellowship is encouraged to so organize that all evangelical organizations in the national area may be allowed to join and that individuals who find themselves involved with organizations related to the ecumenical movement may as individuals find fellowship in the national body. It has been suggested since the merger of the IMC with the World Council of Churches that organizations desiring to cooperate with a national fellowship or alliance should not at the same time be organically related to the WCC. Naturally, however, this is left for a final decision to each national entity which will determine its own policies.

II

Currently we face problems in this over-all area. These occur mainly at two levels. First of all, there already exists in Latin America a number of councils, alliances, federations and fellowships that, in order to gain national cooperation, agreed not to relate themselves to anything else outside the country. This was readily agreed to — first by the evangelicals themselves because they did not want to get involved in the World Council of Churches and, secondly, by those favorable to the WCC who had nothing to lose since their affiliation with the world organization was through their denomination rather than an alliance or federation.

This gave the latter groups a weapon, however, to keep evangelicals from affiliating with the World Evangelical Fellowship since this membership is at the national organizational level rather than by denominations. Moreover, it is interesting to note in Latin America, for example, that two denominations are famous as "joiners" — the United Presbyterian Church and the Methodist Church. In every case where there has been a move, even though started by evangelicals in an area to tie themselves together, they immediately found the Methodists or Presbyterians or both waiting at the door to join.

Virtually all of these fellowships have a statement of faith and I know of specific instances where these groups were willing to sign it even though they admitted they were not quite in agreement with it. They just allow themselves the right to interpret the meaning of the terms in the statement. The evangelicals are well aware that it is practically impossible to preserve theological or doctrinal purity in any organization by the simple expedient of using a statement of faith. Thus these agencies which cannot relate themselves to anything outside the country become an actual obstacle in international evangelical fellowship and unity.

It is probably not too much to say that it is almost inevitable that these fellowships will eventually break up or will be supplemented by a strictly evangelical fellowship if we are to see our evangelical unity implemented in all these countries around the world.

This should not be construed to mean that evangelicals want to be exclusive. Their drive is positive in that they want to pull people together, not simply for purposes at the organizational level, but because they believe it is incumbent upon us to bring together those true evangelicals whether they are in or out of the World Council of Churches. They do not want to be organically related to the WCC.

In other countries such as Africa where there is no problem of relationships, i.e., the councils can join if they want to, another disturbing factor has entered. The World Council of Churches is operating through its members who, as missionary sending agencies from North America or Europe, are holding membership in councils or federations which are not related to the WCC. This provides the means of infiltrating these countries with the ecumenical message and drive. This is being done mainly through specialized conferences for youth, conferences on education, conferences on social and economic revolution, and such meetings as the All-Africa Church Conference which is an organization of the WCC to try to pull the African churches into one continental body. The inevitable result of this drive will be the break-up of these councils and evangelicals will be forced to withdraw and establish their own fellowships to replace previous ties.

On the continent there is a peculiarly and exclusively evangelical problem. Where the old evangelical alliances have practically ceased to function, they are still legally in existence with sometimes only one or two strong leaders. These in turn have by their existence effectively blocked the establishment of a more dynamic evangelical fellowship. These are problems that will need to be worked out in each country where there are still strong evangelical constituencies. Like the Evangelical Alliance in England, these will very likely be set up on an individual membership basis.

Evangelicals are making advances through the World Evangelical Fellowship. A complete re-evaluation of its functions and constitution was made in Hong Kong in 1962. It still is in need of implementing much of its program through its commissions and regional offices, but progress is being made. An Asian office has been authorized. A world office now functions out of London with a general secretary. New fellowships are being organized. In 1962 fellowships were formed in Sierra Leone and the Ivory Coast in West Africa. A new fellowship is in the making in the Rhodesias.

More recently a joint African office has been established in Nairobi, Kenya, with the cooperation of the Interdenominational Foreign Missions Association, the Evangelical Foreign Missions Association, and the Evangelical Missionary Alliance of England. A full-time director who knows the African situation will soon be joined by an African associate. The main purpose of this office is to encourage and promote cooperation among evangelicals at the national and later the international level.

In like manner efforts are being made to encourage cooperation among evangelicals in Latin America and backing is being given to an organization that the Latin Americans themselves have established, known as the Committee in Latin America for Evangelism. It is also known to us that in several Latin American countries efforts are being made to pull the evangelicals together for cooperation at the national level.

III

Finally, what is our strategy in implementing our evangelical unity? The key word at this level is that it must be a spiritual program. The only hope for success in manifesting a spiritual oneness before the world is through the indwelling presence of the Holy Spirit and His control upon the church.

Keeping this in mind, there are several things that can be done. The fellowships and alliances now in existence in many countries can encourage pastors' retreats for spiritual renewal and revitalization in the work for an increase of vision and enthusiasm in carrying forward the Great Commission.

Another practical implementation can be united efforts at evangelism. Although every national church and mission is encouraged to do its utmost in evangelism, it is recognized that at the cooperative level efforts at saturation evangelism — or as it is called in Latin America, "Evangelism in Depth" — can be effective. This not only produces results in the spread of the Gospel, but serves as a marvelous vehicle to demonstrate our spiritual oneness in Christ.

Evangelicals are now giving dynamic leadership in the field of missionary radio. In addition, cooperative efforts in the production of literature have also proven most effective.

One of the ultimate purposes of these fellowships is precisely to offer fellowship to the various churches and groups in any one nation. We in America have a tendency to forget that in most cases evangelicals are a very small minority and virtually lost in the midst of a great pagan culture. It is vitally necessary that these people be brought into relationship with one another to realize that they do not stand alone in the midst of the great whitened harvest which confronts them.

The zenith of this fellowship is reached when internationally those who are of like mind and faith, although not necessarily totally uniform in their theological belief and emphasis, can get together and find that in Christ they are one. This offers incredible encouragement and satisfaction to these faithful servants of Christ. Thus at the continental level and the international level it is hoped that these fellowships can be brought together that we might unitedly make a spiritual stand in this day for the completion of the task that confronts us.

Chapter Eight

UNION OR UNITY — THE PRESENT DAY DILEMMA

George L. Ford

There is one verse in the Bible that the ecumenical movement takes at face value — or more. While many of the leaders may question other portions of Scripture, they are sure of this one. They may criticize evangelicals for being too literal in interpreting the Bible, but in this case they are more literal than any biblicist ever thought of being. And this is in spite of the fact that both the content and the context of the verse indicate that its principal emphasis is spiritual.

I am speaking of John 17:21: "That they all may be one; as thou, Father, art in me, and I in thee, that they also may be one in us; that the world may believe that thou hast sent me." Marcellus Kik suggests that this "has become the charter of the ecumenical movement and finds constant repetition in all of its literature."[1]

This brings us face to face with the question of whether Christ's prayer in the garden was for union or unity. Was its main thrust for an outward organizational manifestation or for an inner and spiritual unity upon which true Christian cooperation could be built? It is my belief that while Christ desires the manifestation of unity before the world, it must first of all be spiritual and inner if it is to have any validity in representing Christ to a world lost in sin.

The historical development of Christian cooperation has already been traced in preceding chapters. It has been clearly pointed out that until fairly recent years there has always been a creedal basis for Christian cooperation. This certainly would appear to be necessary, for whatever else Christian cooperation becomes, it must be thoroughly Christian. There must also be some means of defining what we mean by "Christian."

This was adequately cared for in the early days of unity efforts. Evangelicals did the pioneering and they were careful that doctrinal purity was not relegated to a position of secondary importance. Those who start their historical considerations with the World Missionary Conference of 1910 miss the fact that evangelicals charted the course more than half-a-century prior to that with the founding of the Evangelical Alliance in 1846. By 1910 the liberals had already brought dissension and discord into the cooperative movement by withdrawing from the Alliance in 1894 and setting up their own organization. Josiah Strong, one of the leaders of the Alliance, helped to sabotage that organization because it would not adopt his new concept of the social gospel.

All of this points out clearly that there is no disagreement beween the evangelical and the ecumenist concerning the desirability — nor indeed the necessity — of Christian unity. The question is whether unity shall be based on an outward organizational form that is fully realizable only through organic merger, or if it is to be a basic spiritual unity which manifests itself in love, consideration and cooperation with others who share like precious faith.

Some question whether the purpose of the ecumenical movement is to achieve organizational union. This really cannot be doubted if one follows very closely the publications of the movements involved and the writings of the leaders. A few references here should be adequate.

Dr. Charles C. Morrison, founder and long-time editor of *The Christian Century* as well as an early ecumenical leader, wrote in *The Unfinished Reformation:* "Those who guide the movement hesitate frankly to suggest that its goal would necessarily involve some adjustment, if not radical abandonment, of the denominational system."[2]

Dr. Peter Brunner, professor of systematic theology at the University of Heidelberg, Germany, says, "We dare not lose sight of the goal of the ecumenical movement! This goal is a full union of our divided churches. We must now travel new roads which will bring us closer to this goal."[3]

Bishop Lesslie Newbigin of the Church of South India suggests in *Is Christ Divided?* that there is no difference between the "ideal" and the "real" church. Building on this premise he states that "the disunity of the church is the denial of the promise and a contradiction of the purpose for which the church was sent into the world.

. . . The divisions of the church are a public denial of the sufficiency of the atonement. . . . When we have understood God's purpose for the church as it is shown in the Scriptures, there is only one thing to do about our divisions; it is to repent of them, to go — all of us — humbly to the mercy seat and ask the Lord Himself to show us where we have gone wrong and what we must do to end this scandal."[4]

Dr. Paul Griswold Macy, former secretary of the American Committee for the World Council of Churches, has written a very readable history of the WCC under the title *If It Be of God.* Early in the book he describes the Church Universal as the sum total of all local, regional and national church bodies. Near the end he states that the thing the early church started out to do was to "hold the world together." In between is his story of the organization that builds on the organizational concepts of the church to accomplish its earthbound social purposes.

It is interesting to note Dr. Macy's emphasis of the fact that as early as 1938 the International Missionary Council, which spawned the commissions that led to the organization of the World Council of Churches, adopted a statement asserting that "visible and organic union must be our goal."[5]

Faith and Order Trend, the quarterly publication of the Department of Faith and Order Study of the National Council of Churches, which describes itself as a journal for "furthering the interdenominational promotion of faith and order program of the World Council of Churches," presents some interesting information along this line in its issue of December, 1962.

The lead article relates to the Week of Prayer for Christian Unity which was begun by the WCC in 1962. It might be well to point out here that the Evangelical Alliance started a prayer observance in 1846 known as the Universal Week of Prayer, held the first week of the new year, which is still carried on in many nations under evangelical sponsorship.

The article in *Faith and Order Trend* points out that some of the outstanding achievements in the first attempt in 1962 related to the bringing together of Catholic and Protestant leaders in prayer and consultation. It comments that "acts of Christian unity such as this play an important part in bringing the ecumenical movement out of the circle of specialists into the wider circle of the universal Christian family." This week of prayer for Christian unity was set so that it coincides with the Roman Catholic observance of an annual week of prayer between the feasts of St. Peter's chair at Rome and the feast of the conversion of St. Paul. Dolores McCahill, religion editor of the *Chicago Sun-Times,* wrote that "The Council . . . was looking around for some expression of interest in unity on the part of Catholics to which it could forge at least an invisible link."[6]

Although *Faith and Order Trend* is only a 12-page quarterly bulletin, one full page is given to the development in the United States and around the world of merger movements between denominations. Beyond this it must be said that the major editorial content seems to point in this direction.

There is no question but that the real thrust of the ecumenical movement is "one church for one world." For one who accepts the theory of the organizational nature of the church, there is hardly any other choice.

Frankly, I cannot accept this position. I cannot conceive that the true Church of Christ is synonymous with the sum total of all church organizational life. Something of the true nature of the church is stated by Paul in Acts 20:28. Speaking to the elders of the church at Ephesus he admonishes them "to feed the church of God, which he hath purchased with his own blood." The true Church is composed of those who have been redeemed by the blood of Christ. This must include not only the fact of the provision of the blood of Christ, but the application of His blood in cleansing power to the heart of the repentant sinner who is transformed into a rejoicing believer. Such a person is a part of the body of Christ and is one with every other true believer.

Now the real issue is this: If the objective is the union of all churches, what does this do to the unity of faith? Must I cast away my belief that salvation is by grace through faith and not through the church so that I may be one with the Roman Catholic Church? Must I replace my faith in the authority of the Scriptures with a faith in the scientific approach so I can be one with the liberal who feels he must accommodate his faith to the culture of the day?

Recently there came to my attention a sermon by a Methodist pastor in California in which he makes a systematic effort to destroy

faith in the virgin birth of Christ and to discount the teachings of
Scripture. Am I to ignore his departure from the historical, evangelical, Biblical position and minimize the differences of faith in
order that I may manifest an outward form of unity?

The official policy of the Russian Orthodox Church states: "The
Orthodox clergy and laity are utterly loyal to the Soviet power. We
are Russians. Our religion is Russia's national religion." Must I
renounce my conviction that the real source of Soviet power — to
which this church pledges its loyalty — is Satan himself so I can be
one with the members of that church?

Marcellus Kik has well said, "Organizational union without
concord in doctrine will fail to impress the observant world."[7]

We must remember that the work of the church is achieved not
by strength of numbers or organizational might, but by the ministry
of the Holy Spirit through the lives of yielded believers. Organizational union is not the real answer to the need for Christian unity.

Now this does not mean that evangelicals are necessarily opposed to all church mergers. There are cases where churches have
merged with beneficial results. There are others where it well could
be done. First of all, however, there must be a unity of faith or the
unity of form is a mere sham. When faith is surrendered to organization and conviction is replaced by a desire to create a good image,
you no longer have a representation of the true Church of God but
a paganized church that has turned to worship the gods of man's
own making.

What then is the answer? How shall we work together for the
fulfillment of the prayer of Christ for Christian unity?

First we must start from the clear truth of John 17:21. I would
not deny the implications of the outward manifestation of Christian
unity in this verse. I do strongly believe that no one who ap-
proaches this verse with genuine scholarship can dig from it the
meaning that is applied by some of the leaders of the ecumenical
movement. This is especially true if it is considered in the context
of the entire chapter. There is no suggestion here of the achieve-
ment of Christian unity by organizational or mechanical methods.
In fact, when Christ said, "As thou, Father, art in me, and I in
thee . . ." He was making it very clear that the basis of Christian
unity is spiritual. He prayed specifically that this would be the

standard for the unity which would be known and manifested among His followers.

The purpose of unity is also made very clear in this verse. It is ". . . that the world may believe that thou hast sent me." This cannot be harmonized with the liberal concept that Christ is man become God. He is rather God become man. This means that Christ must be revealed to the world in all of His reality and power as the virgin-born Son of God who lived a sinless life, died an atoning death, rose from the grave, ascended into heaven and is coming again to receive His own unto Himself.

The unity of the faith must include at least this much. Unless it does, church union does not accomplish the purpose for which Christ prayed but merely provides an arena in which the conflicts continue.

Evangelical efforts in Christian cooperation have always been based on a unity of faith. We feel that the statement of faith which was adopted when the National Association of Evangelicals was started is essential for building any true Christian unity. This does not mean that it would have to be stated in exactly the same words, but the concept of biblical authority, the nature and work of Christ, the necessity of a transforming experience of the individual through the power of God, the work of the Holy Spirit in the life of the believer must be part and parcel of any cooperative effort that is thoroughly and genuinely Christian.

Evangelicals are sometimes accused of being negative in their approach. In reality, not only have they been the pioneers in Christian cooperation, but they have always taken a positive Biblical position. The ecumenical movement is basically negative in its approach as it relates to the Word of God. Its creed is social rather than theological. It is "ecumenical" not only in the sense that it is worldwide, but also in the sense that it is limited to this world.

But there must be more than a unity of faith. There must also be a unity of fellowship. One of the most rewarding experiences of evangelicals is to come together with others who may be from different church backgrounds and yet who have come to know Christ as personal Saviour. There is a bond of oneness here that membership in one organization — or even in one family — cannot match. It is a oneness of spiritual depth because we have been made one through the blood of Christ. We actually experience the unity for which Christ prayed in His high-priestly intercession. We are not simply one in each other nor do we become one by submerging our interests in a common organizational thrust. We are one in Christ!

But genuine Christian unity has another dimension. This is found in the outreach of Christian love to the lost. Much has been said about the brotherhood of man and the fatherhood of God. In the general sense this is admittedly true because we all come from one common creation of God and share a human brotherhood. But in the spiritual sense we are not all brothers because not all have been born into the spiritual family of God. Thus it was that Christ referred to some whose father was the devil (John 8:42-44).

Knowing this and knowing that we were all once the children of Satan, our concern must be to bring other men into the spiritual unity we have found in Christ. This means the preaching of the saving power of the blood of Christ which is able to wash away sin and transform the life.

Dr. Kik declares that "a church that refuses to declare what is vital for salvation under the pretext of achieving unity is both cowardly and unfaithful to her God-given mission of being a pillar for truth. . . . The scandal of the ecumenical movement is ignoring the blood of Christ as the means by which men are reconciled to God and brought into unity one with another."[8]

God forbid that we would lose sight of the unity of our mission in the proclamation of the saving power of the blood of Christ in this day.

Chapter Nine

EVANGELICALS – DIVISIVE OR DYNAMIC?

W. Stanley Mooneyham

Two small boys were playing with a wagon one day. They were each trying to ride at the same time, but there was little evident enjoyment. Finally one of the youngsters turned to the other and said, "You know, one of us could have lot more fun if you would get off."

There are probably more than a few who fervently wish that evangelicals would adopt the philosophy of that little story and thus solve what has been called the most pressing problem facing the churches today — "the scandal of our divisions." All it would take to usher in the ecumenical millennium is for evangelicals to get down off their high-horse and on the bandwagon—and there are many church leaders who can't understand why we persist on being so uncooperative.

Don't we know that the church is in crisis? Aren't we aware that "our divided churches, all more and more sectarian in fact, are all therefore less and less Christian in influence"? Can't we see that the exploding population is increasing the number of pagans to Christian disciples to an alarming ratio — presently 13 to one, but destined to become 50 to one by the year 2,000? And don't we know that cooperation really isn't enough and that the only way to make governments listen to the church and the world respect its power is to have a united body?

Some of our ecumenical friends wait most impatiently for the answers. Now and again in their frustration they tag us with such uncomplimentary labels as "apostles of discord." Of course, the immediate human reaction is to throw up your defense and swing a retaliatory punch all at the same time. And whatever else we are, we *are* human. So we think up a choice rejoinder, call the whole crowd a bunch of "ecumaniacs," and with a smirk of self-satisfaction dust off our hands and return to tending our flocks.

But somehow I don't think we can escape the responsibility of an honest soul-searching that easily. What *is* the truth about us? Are we really discordant in our harmony, disagreeable in our manner, divisive in our methods? And let us not answer hastily.

We dare not sit as judge and jury on ourselves. Let the Holy Spirit judge our often fragmented witness in the light of Paul's assertion that "we are laborers together with God" (I Corinthians 3:9). Let the apostle's question, "Is Christ divided?" (I Corinthians 1:13) speak to the fleshly-motivated schisms of our time. Let the words of the Master, "This is my commandment, That ye love one another, as I have loved you" (John 15:2) rebuke the loveless orthodoxy which makes it possible for His disciples to bite and devour one another.

I think the Holy Spirit will not let us escape the fact that our preaching of Christian unity is in some instances far ahead of our practice of it. It is not as though we had already attained. There are yet scores of ways in which our spiritual unity needs to be — and can be — made visible.

But does this mean that evangelicals are the divisive element in Christendom today? Is our fidelity to doctrine to be construed as plain pigheadedness when we are constantly told that doctrine divides while service unites? What can we answer when face to face on the trail Ahab asks Elijah, "Art thou he that troubleth Israel?" (I Kings 18:17).

Let me give you a study in contrasts. Perhaps it will help answer the question.

For the first scene we have to go to the campus of the University of Michigan at Ann Arbor. The time is August, 1961. Gathered on the campus are nearly 2,000 young people from 40 different denominations who are attending the North American Ecumenical Youth Assembly.

Here a great to-do was made over the scandal of the division of Christendom. One of the speakers — a Burmese Baptist layman — declared that "Christians who cannot break bread together, or drink the cup of fellowship, renew the scars of His (Christ's) body and tear asunder His image." To illustrate his point a veil picturing the face of Christ was cut apart publicly and each piece was given to representatives of various denominations as a graphic object lesson of their divided state.

On the opening night the young people were visibly reminded that a joint communion service could not be held by the shining of a spotlight upon an empty chalice around which an interpretive dance was staged.[1]

A news release from one of the sponsoring groups just ahead of the conference asked if it were possible to "awaken the same sense of shame in Christian youth of today" which young ecumenists had in the early days of the movement. I don't know whether or not they succeeded, but I know that at Ann Arbor they made a serious, calculated effort.

For the next scene let us go to the University of Illinois at Urbana just five months later. Gathered here are over 5,000 students coming from every state in the union and 50 foreign countries. They are giving up part of their Christmas holiday to attend the sixth International Student Missionary Convention sponsored by Inter-Varsity Christian Fellowship.

They represent as diverse theological backgrounds as you can possibly imagine. I talked with a young Negro Pentecostal girl from Colorado, a Greek Orthodox engineering student from Lebanon, an Anglican divinity student from Uganda, a Southern Baptist boy from Oklahoma, an Egyptian pastor of the only Protestant church in tiny Kuwait. I lived in a dormitory room with some of them — got up for their early morning Bible study, stayed up for their late night prayer meetings.

I felt their spiritual heartbeat as they wept and asked God to make them strong witnesses on their campuses. I shared in the undiluted Christian love which they lavished on each other. I sensed the deep moving of the Holy Spirit as He pressed the claims of Jesus Christ upon each of them.

And I watched with a tremendous swelling pride as by the scores and hundreds they made the full commitment of life to the Lord who had saved them. Nearly 400 of them definitely committed themselves for missionary service — another 900 pledged to seek God's will about it.

As the clock struck midnight to usher in the new year on the last night of the convention, the fieldhouse where they were meeting became a holy sanctuary as they sat down together — some 5,000 of them — and under the leadership of an Anglican bishop from Australia joined in a communion service to share the emblems representing the body and blood of their Lord.

There was no handwringing because they did not all bear the same denominational label. Although they surely were aware of it, it didn't seem to matter — and none of the conference leaders seemed to think that it was important enough at the time to point it out.

I have called this a study in contrasts. At this conference no one mouthed any platitudes about Christian unity; they just went about quietly bearing witness to the oneness which they possessed as disciples of the same Lord.

It is my observation that this is rather characteristic of responsible evangelicalism today. There may not be as much preaching about Christian unity as with some others, but there is more practice of it. There is less pointing out our differences and more pointing up our common fidelity to the Bible and loyalty to Jesus Christ.

You see, harmony is not that sound which is produced by playing just one string on a violin. You don't get harmony by playing one string — you get monotony. Harmony is that pleasing agreement of sounds when all the instruments are playing from the same score and in the same key. Paul described it as "endeavoring to keep the unity of the Spirit in the bond of peace" (Ephesians 4:3). He didn't ask the Ephesians to manufacture unity for he knew the impossibility of fabricating humanly what the Holy Spirit of God must produce supernaturally. They were already together, he reminded them, for "there is one body, and one Spirit . . . one hope . . . one Lord, one faith, one baptism, one God and Father of all . . ." (Ephesians 4:4-6). Their job was to protect the unity which their mutual faith had brought them.

Evangelicals just don't see that corporate union can necessarily be equated with spiritual dynamism. The merging of two half-dead churches does not make one live church. In one chapter of a new book, *The Unity We Seek,* Dr. George Johnston, an ecumenical leader from Canada, mentions that thus far there have been only two types of church unions. These are represented by the United

Church of Canada and the Church of South India. He says, however, that "the latter has been described in ecumenical circles as 'dynamic,' because it involves much more radically the death and resurrection of the denominations that enter it."[2]

Or to put it another way, the more successfully you commit suicide, the more dynamic you are — a bit of logic that is open to question.

At the heart of the evangelical movement today are three of the most dynamic elements the world has ever known. They constitute its genius. And let me say that far from being a corpse that lies between its last breath and rigor mortis, evangelicalism is and intends to remain vigorously alive. Check any of the areas of church life which you will that are valid for spiritual measurements — evangelism, Sunday schools, stewardship, missions — and you will find that it is the evangelical churches which bear the signs of life and growth.

The first of these elements that gives the evangelical movement its dynamic is the Bible, the Word of God. This is the foundation upon which the whole body, fitly framed together, rises. This is the launching pad against which our thrust is generated. This is home plate where we firmly plant our feet.

There are those who will not give the Bible this place. When an airplane made its first appearance many years ago over a little town in Mississippi, one of the local fellows watched it for a bit and then turned away shaking his head. Someone asked him what was wrong. "If that engine ever stops, the pilot sure is in trouble," he said. "There ain't no place for him to stand to crank it."

He had a point—and I think this rather precisely illustrates the predicament of those who refuse an authoritative Bible. It is hard to be dynamic when you have nothing solid on which to stand. Those who do not have a Bible which speaks to human need with authority cannot assuredly thunder, "Thus said the Lord!" The very best they can do is weakly suggest that the person take the Bible and see if perhaps God might break through the print and speak to the point of his need.

The Bible is a dynamic instrument. When J. B. Phillips was translating the New Testament epistles he remarked that while he did not hold fundamentalist views on "inspiration," he was continually struck by the living quality of the material on which he was working. "Some will, no doubt, consider it merely superstitious reverence for 'Holy Writ,'" he said, "yet again and again the writer felt rather like an electrician rewiring an ancient house without being able 'to turn the mains off.'"[3]

The Bible *is* supernatural! It literally pulsates with divine energy. It witnesses of itself that it is "living and active, sharper than any two-edged sword" (Hebrews 4:12, RSV).

When King Arthur lay dying he called one of his knights, Sir Bedivere, to his bed. "Here," he said, "take Excalibur, my sword, and throw it in the lake." This was the sword which had enabled the king to lead his Knights of the Round Table to so many spectacular victories. On his way to the lake, Sir Bedivere admired the sword, especially the dazzling jewels on the handle.

"How foolish to throw away so valuable a treasure. I'll hide it under this tree." And he hurried back to his king.

"What did you see?" Arthur anxiously inquired.

"O, naught but the waves lapping at the shore," the knight told him.

"You lie! Go and do as I said. Throw the sword into the lake."

Sir Bedivere left a second time. He took the sword from under the tree and started for the lake. But he looked again at Excalibur and thought of the great victories it had won. "It is folly and shameful to throw away such a powerful weapon," he reasoned. "It can win many more wonderful victories. The times and I need it."

So he hid it again.

"What did you see?" the king asked when he returned.

"Only the waves gently lapping the shore."

"You lie! Go fling the sword out over the lake. If you don't I'll rise from my bed and slay thee."

This time Sir Bedivere was afraid even to look at the sword lest he be tempted again. With all his might he flung the mighty Excalibur out over the lake. A white, mystic hand rose up out of the water, caught it, and drew it beneath the waves.

The church has been given a divine Excalibur! It is the Word of God, the mighty Sword of the Spirit.

Sometime ago an unprecedented meeting was held in the sports arena in Cali, Columbia. The Roman Catholics had agreed to sponsor a joint meeting with the evangelicals in which leaders of both groups would be free to discuss their beliefs before a public audience. Every one of the 8,000 seats was filled and crowds milled around outside unable to get in. Because Protestants are such a minority in this South American country, the audience was overwhelmingly Roman Catholic.

A Colombian Baptist pastor was the first speaker and his subject was "The Message of the Bible." During his sermon he lifted his Bible high and began to quote the Spanish version of the hymn, "Holy Bible, Book divine; precious treasure, thou art mine." Before he had finished the crowd was on its feet, some were weeping, and a thunderous applause rocked the arena.

At the heart of the evangelical dynamic is the Bible—inspired, infallible, authoritative—and we refuse to be intellectually intimidated by those whose sophistication has caused them to abandon it. Someone once asked Charles Spurgeon if he were all set for the defense of the Bible. "Defend the Bible!" he thundered, "I would as soon defend a lion. The Bible doesn't need to be defended; it needs only to be let loose."

And this suggests the second element which produces the evangelical dynamic—the Gospel of our Lord Jesus Christ, declared by Paul to be "the power of God" (Romans 1:15). This is the Word of God applied, both in pulpit declaration and personal witnessing.

There is dynamite in this message. The early church discovered this. Luke tells us "they that were scattered abroad went everywhere preaching the word" (Acts 8:4). They turned loose the Word of God and it changed society because it changed people.

Early American church history records the thrilling story of a revival that swept up the Appalachian Mountains and literally transformed the state of Kentucky. Logan County in that state had a notorious reputation. It was the refuge for escaped murderers, horse thieves, highway robbers and counterfeiters. People from the East who visited this frontier section were shocked by the swearing, fighting, Sabbath-breaking and lawlessness which prevailed.

But under the zealous and persuasive preaching of James Mc-Gready, a Presbyterian minister of Scotch-Irish descent, a great awakening began which came to be known as the Cumberland

Revival. Peter Cartwright was another preacher of that era. And the Gospel of Christ, faithfully and powerfully preached, wrought a miracle in Logan County. A witness writing to an eastern correspondent described the effect: "I found Kentucky to appearances the most moral place I had ever been. A profane expression was hardly ever heard. A religious awe seemed to pervade this country. . . ."

And as the frontier swept westward, still these faithful preachers went everywhere applying the dynamic of the Gospel to the social problems of the day. As the work of home missions and church extension challenged the missionary conscience of the people, new churches were established in every outpost and the power of God continued to be released through the preaching of these missionaries.

One such pioneer was C. C. McCabe, a Methodist home missionary. One day while traveling on a train he noticed a newspaper report which stirred him deeply. The celebrated infidel, Robert G. Ingersoll, had told a free-thinkers convention in New York that "the churches are dying out all over the land."

McCabe got off the train at the next station to dispatch a telegram which read: "Dear Robert: All hail the power of Jesus' name, we are building more than one Methodist church for every day in the year, and propose to make it two a day. Signed, C. C. McCabe."

Well, the Methodists rejoiced in this incident and soon found themselves singing this little song:

> The infidels, a motley band,
>   In council met and said:
> "The churches die through all the land,
>   The last will soon be dead."
> When suddenly a message came,
>   It filled them with dismay:
> "All hail the power of Jesus' name,
>   We're building two a day!"

When the unchanging, unlimited power of God is released through the preaching of the Gospel, night *must* give way to day! And this is the only power the church has to turn back the tide of paganism which threatens to engulf the world. It will never be done by any number of social betterment societies. In the final analysis, the best they can do is put a veneer of culture on the pagan. It takes the dynamic of the Gospel to change the human heart.

There is a third dynamic element at work in evangelicalism today—and that is the power of prevailing prayer. I will grant you that there isn't enough prayer in anybody's church today, but heaven's resources are still available to us when we tap them through prayer. Prayer is not simply a futile exercise and it is more than a pretty ritual. James speaks of it as a working force: "The earnest prayer of a righteous man makes tremendous power available—dynamic in its working" (James 5:16b, *Amplified*).

In 1962 the city of Denver faced a crime wave which many felt was the result of a demoralizing police scandal that had rocked the town. The chief of police appealed through the newspapers for public support in Denver's fight against underworld elements. Houston Gibson, an evangelical layman whose auto supply firm had been burglarized three times, was determined to do something about Chief James Slavin's plea. A telephone call to Dr. Russell Ayres Pavy, president of the Denver Association of Evangelicals, and a subsequent conference with the mayor resulted in an official call for a special inter-faith week of prayer.

Committees under the leadership of evangelicals secured the cooperation of every major faith and led the city in prayer. Denver prayed! Publicly and privately, in the churches and on the steps of City Hall, at a mayor's prayer breakfast and in family groups— Denver prayed.

The chief of police said, "If our society has not become completely conditioned to cynicism, who is to say that through an earnest, sincere repenting appeal to our Father we may witness a miraculous improvement in the moral standards and values of our fellow citizens and in each one of us who go to the Lord in prayer?"

Few in Denver would dispute Chief Slavin's words. They saw such a miraculous improvement—for during the five-day period immediately following the week of prayer, the only crime reported in either of Denver's two newspapers was the theft of a bicycle! Some will call it sheer coincidence, but others of us who haven't been demythologized cannot help believe that God in heaven heard

— and answered — the prayers of His believing and concerned children.

I am more than a little disturbed about how we depreciate the tremendous power of prayer. In the book of Acts we are told how immediately after the coming of the Holy Spirit, the early church went through a deep valley of testing. Two of its strongest leaders were thrown into prison and threatened for preaching that Jesus had risen from the dead. And do you know what they did upon their release? They returned to the little congregation and reported the threat; they described the dark cloud of opposition rising against the infant church; they faced squarely this hour of crisis—and then they went to prayer!

They didn't call a strategy meeting or a business meeting. They called a prayer meeting. As a result, God did something wonderful. Acts 4 tells the story. "And when they had prayed, the place was shaken where they were assembled together; and they were all filled with the Holy Ghost . . ." (v. 31). That fresh visitation of the Holy Spirit upon the church assembled produced three things that for us today can mean the difference between humiliating defeat and glorious victory.

The first thing was a love-inspired fellowship: "And the multitude of them that believed were of one heart and of one soul" (v. 32). This was more than a shallow togetherness; it was a dynamic fellowship fused by the melting power of the Holy Spirit in human hearts. There is strength—God's strength—in that kind of oneness.

Something else happened after that prayer meeting, too. The apostles preached with new power: "And with great power gave the apostles witness of the resurrection of the Lord Jesus" (v. 33). Power in preaching doesn't come from a homiletics class; it comes when the Holy Spirit actually possesses the heart and soul of the preacher. When Jonathan Edwards preached someone said it was as though he were walking up and down the village streets pointing his accusing finger "at one house after another, uncovering secret sins and holding them up for all to see."

It is this kind of excited, turbulent, desperate preaching which has characterized the church in its finest hours. Let us plead with heaven: "Do it again, Lord! Do it again!"

The third result of the outpouring of the Holy Spirit on that prayer meeting was a stewardship revival that surpasses anything the church has ever seen since. All those who possessed houses or land sold them and gave everything to God (v. 34). Total consecration invaded that assembly and Barnabas of Cyprus so caught the blessing that he sold out completely to the Lord.

Phillips translates it, "A wonderful spirit of generosity pervaded the whole fellowship." They had caught a vision. They were living beyond themselves. They had been charged and fired with the heart-throb of God and nothing would be withheld in the urgent task of speeding the Gospel to the world.

This is the strategy that evangelicals need today—the linking up of our churches with tasks that challenge them to utmost sacrifice. Woven into the very fabric of our convictions is the dynamic to do the job Christ has commissioned us to do. He now stands just down the corridor of history-yet-to-be, encouraging us to dedication and faithfulness. And waiting for our response.

REFERENCES

Chapter One

1. Cited in *The Christian Century*, November 1, 1961, p. 1306.
2. Cited in *Information Service*, February 16, 1963, p. 2.
3. Cited in Henry Cook, *The Theology of Evangelism* (London: The Carey Kingsgate Press, Ltd., 1951), p. 112.
4. J. Robert Nelson, *The Realm of Redemption* (Chicago: Cloister Press, Wilcox and Follett Co., 1951), p. 202.
5. cf. Ernest Best, *One Body in Christ* (London: SPCK, 1955), p. 8.
6. *Ibid.*, p. 189.
7. *Ibid.*, p. 197.
8. J. Marcellus Kik, *Ecumenism and the Evangelical* (Philadelphia: The Presbyterian and Reformed Publishing Company, 1958), pp. 100-101.
9. *Ibid.*, p. 102.
10. *Ibid.*, p. 106.
11. Cited in Kik, *op. cit.*, p. 71.
12. *Loc. cit.*
13. Nelson, *op. cit.*, pp. 204-205.
14. Cited in Kik, *op. cit.*, p. 95.
15. Cited in William E. Barton, *The Law of the Congregational Usage* (Chicago: Advance Publishing Company, 1916), p. 62.
16. Charles Hodge, *Essays and Reviews* (New York: Robert Carter and Brothers, 1879), pp. 207-208.
17. Oscar Cullman, "The Early Church and the Ecumenical Problem," *Anglican Theological Review*, Vol. XL, No. 3, July, 1958, p. 188.
18. Emil Brunner, *The Christian Doctrine of the Church, Faith, and the Consummation* (Philadelphia: The Westminster Press, 1962), pp. 127-128.
19. Nelson, *op. cit.*, pp. 209-210.

Chapter Two

1. S. L. Greenslade, *Schism in the Early Church* (London: SCM Press Ltd., 1953), p. 22.
2. *Ibid.*, p. 32.
3. Geoffrey Grimshaw Willis, *Saint Augustine and the Donatist Controversy* (London: SPCK, 1950), p. 38.
4. Colin W. Williams, *John Wesley's Theology Today* (New York: Abingdon Press, 1960), p. 146.

5. Robert W. Burtner and Robert E. Chiles, Eds., *A Compend of Wesley's Theology* (New York: Abingdon Press, 1954), p. 257.
6. "John Wesley's Changing Concept of the Ministry," *Religion in Life,* Spring, 1962, p. 270.
7. *Loc. cit.*
8. Greenslade, *op. cit.*, p. 32 n. 45.
9. *Ibid.,* pp. 110, 111.
10. Geoffrey F. Nuttall, *Visible Saints, the Congregational Way 1640-1660* (Oxford: Blackwell, 1957), p. 59.
11. Greenslade, *op. cit.*, p. 38.
12. Cited in Edward John Carnell, *The Case for Orthodox Theology* (Philadelphia: Westminster Press, 1959), p. 136.
13. Cited Willis, *op. cit.*, pp. 96-97, 100-101.
14. Carnell, *op. cit.*, p. 133.
15. C. C. Goen, *Revivalism and Separation in New England,* 1740-1800 (New Haven: Yale University Press, 1962), p. 99.
16. Willis, *op. cit.*, pp. 125-126.
17. Nuttall, *op. cit.*, p. 62.
18. *Loc. cit.*, p. 62.
19. Robert C. Walton, *The Gathered Community* (London: Carey Kingsgate Press, 1946), p. 180.
20. E. H. Broadbent, *The Pilgrim Church* (London: Pickering and Inglis, 1931), p. 368.
21. Auguste LeCerf, *An Introduction to Reformed Dogmatics* (London: Lutterworth Press, 1949), pp. 357-358.
22. *Ibid.,* pp. 359, 360, 362.
23. *Ibid.,* pp. 355-356.
24. Greenslade, *op. cit.*, pp. 204-206.

Chapter Three

1. *Sunday School Times,* March 24, 1962.
2. J. Marcellus Kik, *Ecumenism and the Evangelical* (Philadelphia: The Presbyterian and Reformed Publishing Company, 1958), p. 36.
3. *Sunday School Times,* October 20, 1962.
4. Kik, *op. cit.*, p. 136.
5. W. Curry Mavis, *Beyond Conformity* (Winona Lake, Indiana: Light and Life Press, 1958), p. 55.
6. *Ibid.,* p. 74.

Chapter Four

1. Clement, I Corinthians 44, 62.
2. Ignatius, Ephesians 2.
3. Ignatius, Trallians 3, Smyrnaeans 8.
4. Ignatius, Philadelphians 4.
5. Ignatius, Trallians 9-10, Smyrnaeans 2.
6. Irenaeus, *Against Heresies,* IV:ii:2.
7. Tertullians, *De Prescriptione Haereticorum,* XXI.

Chapter Five

1. Theodore Wedel, *The Coming Great Church* (New York: 1945), p. 43.
2. Charles Foster, *An Errand of Mercy* (Chapel Hill, N. C.: 1960), p. 33.
3. Acts 1:4-8, 17:2-3; Romans 10:17-18; I Corinthians 9:16, 14:3-5.
4. *Christianity Today*, March 30, 1962.
5. W. A. Visser't Hooft, *The Pressure of Our Common Calling* (Garden City, N. Y.: 1949), p.

Chapter Six

1. Evangelical Fellowship — Vol. X, No. 4, 1962 — E.F.I. New Delhi, p. 11.
2. Rev. Kenneth Slack, Secretary British Council of Churches, "Dispatch from New Delhi", p. 79.
3. Evangelical Fellowship — Vol. X, No. 4, 1962 — New Delhi, p. 9.
4. African Evangelical Office Report — 12th February, 1963.
5. "Evangelicals and the Evangelical Movement," Leith Samuel, Evangelical Alliance, London, 1962.

Chapter Eight

1. J. Marcellus Kik, *Ecumenism and th Evangelical* (Philadelphia: The Presbyterian and Reformed Publishing Company, 1958), p. 41.
2. Charles C. Morrison, *The Unfinished Reformation* (New York: Harper and Brothers, Publishers, 1953), p. 49.
3. Peter Brunner, *The Unity of the Church — a Symposium*, p. 11.
4. Lesslie Newbigin, *Is Christ Divided?* (Grand Rapids: Eerdmans Publishing Company, 1961), pp. 9-10.
5. Paul Griswold Macy, *If It Be of God* (St. Louis, Bethany Press), p. 43.
6. *Chicago-Sun Times*, January 19, 1963.
7. Kik, *op. cit.*, p.
8. *Ibid.*, pp. 16, 118.

Chapter Nine

1. *United Evangelical Action*, October, 1961.
2. William S. Morris, editor, *The Unity We Seek* (New York: Oxford University Press, 1963), p. 49.
3. J. B. Phillips, *Letters to Young Churches* (London: The Macmillan Company, 1947).

DATE DUE

APR 20 '76			
MAY 13 '76			
Fall 79 Reserve			
SPRING '8' RESERVE			
OCT 13 '82			
MAY 2 '84			

DEMCO 38-297